POPE FRANCIS

SPEAKS TO THE
UNITED STATES AND CUBA

Speeches, Homilies, and Interviews

~

Our Sunday Visitor Publishing Division
Our Sunday Visitor, Inc.
Huntington, Indiana 46750

Copyright © 2015 by Our Sunday Visitor Publishing Division, Our Sunday Visitor, Inc. Published 2015

20 19 18 17 16 15   1 2 3 4 5 6 7 8 9

ISBN: 978-1-68192-019-1 (Inventory No. T1778)
eISBN: 978-1-68192-020-7
LCCN: 2015955513

Cover design: Lindsey Riesen
Cover art: Newscom.com

PRINTED IN THE UNITED STATES OF AMERICA

Contents

FOREWORD

Pope Francis' historic visit to the United States was an apostolic tour de force. From the first images of him descending from the plane at Joint Base Andrews military facility in Maryland and getting into his black Fiat 500L to the final Mass in Philadelphia before almost one million people, the pope from the "ends of the earth" captured the attention of our nation.

Most immediately arresting were the images: The first pope to speak to the U.S. Congress, flanked by a Catholic vice president and a Catholic speaker of the House; the embrace of Sophia Cruz, the little girl who broke through security for a papal hug; the slow drive through the throngs in Central Park in New York; the encounter with the prisoners at Curran-Fromhold prison in Philadelphia; the visit with the homeless at a Catholic Charities shelter.

The 24/7 news coverage feasted on these images and more, and Catholics and non-Catholics alike were transfixed. The visual media culture of the United States meshed with a pope who is keenly aware that he often preaches most eloquently through his actions and gestures. Stroking the face of a handicapped child communicates the abounding mercy of God more directly than a hundred homilies.

Yet what can be lost in the tumult of images is that his words were both profound and pastorally arresting. Take his first sentences to Congress:

> *I am most grateful for your invitation to address this joint session of Congress in 'the land of the free and the home of the brave.' I would like to think that the reason for this is that I too am a son of this great continent, from which we have all received so much and toward which we share a common responsibility.*

Invoking a cherished American self-descriptor — "land of the free and the home of the brave" — the pope established his fellowship with his listeners — "I too am a son of this great continent" — and laid out the essence of his message — gratitude for our blessings and responsibility for what he so often refers to as "our common home."

For the pope, there were always multiple audiences. Not only was he addressing those before whom he stood but also a national and a global audience. Not only was he addressing Catholics, but also the great religious mosaic of America's citizenry, including nonbelievers. This realization shaped his speech. His language in speaking to Congress strove to highlight guiding principles. To the clergy and religious at vespers, his language was more direct and more intimate. And to the prisoners, he was humble and empathetic: *"All of us have something we need to be cleansed of, or purified from. May the knowledge of that fact inspire us to live in solidarity, to support one another and seek the best for others."*

Each of the pope's speeches, both in the United States and in Cuba, merit rereading. The nuances of his message — for example, his reference to religious liberty in his White House address, which is then elaborated on both at the United Nations and in Philadelphia — will become more clear and insightful with each review. At the same time, when the speeches and homilies are taken together, the great themes of this papal visit leap from the page: the care for others, the need for dialogue, the importance of encounter, the condition of the planet, the abundant mercy and providence of God. Pope Francis challenged each one of us: "What about you? What are you going to do?"

In the conclusion of his homily at the Canonization Mass for St. Junipero Serra in Washington, D.C., he exhorts us to rise to the occasion:

Father Serra had a motto which inspired his life and work, a saying he lived his life by: siempre adelante*! Keep moving forward! For him, this was the way to continue experiencing the joy of the Gospel, to keep his heart from growing numb, from being anesthetized. He kept moving forward, because the Lord was waiting.... Today, like him, may we be able to say: Forward! Let's keep moving forward!*

I hope that as you read this volume you underline your favorite passages and write in the margins. I hope you use this opportunity to engage in your own dialogue with Pope Francis, which he so clearly wants. May revisiting these talks deepen your encounter with this humble *pontifex*, this bridge builder, this pastor to the world, as well as to the Savior whose Gospel he preaches without ceasing.

Greg Erlandson
Publisher, Our Sunday Visitor
October 2015

I

Cuba, Point of Encounter

WELCOMING CEREMONY
ADDRESS OF POPE FRANCIS
JOSÉ MARTÍ INTERNATIONAL AIRPORT, HAVANA, CUBA
SATURDAY, SEPTEMBER 19, 2015

~

Mr. President,
Distinguished Authorities,
Brother Bishops,
Ladies and Gentlemen,

I thank you, Mr. President, for your greeting and your kind words of welcome in the name of the government and the entire Cuban people. I also greet the authorities and the members of the diplomatic corps present at this ceremony.

My gratitude also goes to Cardinal Jaime Ortega y Alamino, archbishop of Havana, the Most Reverend Dionisio Guillermo García Ibáñez, archbishop of Santiago de Cuba and president of the episcopal conference, the other bishops, and all the Cuban people, for their warm welcome.

I thank, too, all those who worked to prepare for this pastoral visit. Mr. President, I would ask you to convey my sentiments of particular respect and consideration to your brother Fidel. I would like my greeting to embrace especially all those who, for various reasons, I will not be able to meet, and to Cubans throughout the world.

As you mentioned, Mr. President, this year of 2015 marks the eightieth anniversary of the establishment of sustained diplomatic relations between the Republic of Cuba and the Holy See. Providence today enables me to come to this beloved nation, following the indelible path opened by the unforgettable apostolic journeys which my two predecessors, St. John Paul II and Pope Benedict XVI, made to this island. I know that the memory of those visits awakens gratitude and affection in the people and leaders of Cuba. Today we renew those bonds of cooperation and friendship so that the Church can continue to support and encourage the Cuban people in its hopes and concerns, with the freedom and all the means needed to bring the proclamation of the Kingdom to the existential peripheries of society.

This apostolic journey also coincides with the first centenary of Pope Benedict XV's declaration of Our Lady of Charity of El Cobre as Patroness of Cuba. It was the veterans of the War of Independence who, moved by sentiments of faith and patriotism, wanted the *Virgen mambisa* to be the patroness of Cuba as a free and sovereign nation. Since that time she has accompanied the history of the Cuban people, sustaining the hope which preserves people's dignity in the most difficult situations and championing the promotion of all that gives dignity to the human person. The growing devotion to the Virgin is a visible testimony of her presence in the soul of the Cuban people. In these days I will have occasion to go to El Cobre, as a son and pilgrim, to pray to our Mother for all her Cuban children and for this beloved nation, that it may travel the paths of justice, peace, liberty, and reconciliation.

Geographically, Cuba is an archipelago, facing all directions, with an extraordinary value as a "key" between north and south, east and west. Its natural vocation is to be a point of encounter for all peoples to join in friendship, as José Martí dreamed, "regardless of the languages of isthmuses and the barriers of oceans" (*La Conferencia Monetaria de las Repúblicas de América*, in *Obras escogidas* II, La Habana, 1992, 505). Such was also the desire of St. John Paul II, with his ardent appeal: "May Cuba, with all its magnificent potential, open itself to the world, and may the world open itself to Cuba" (*Arrival Ceremony*, January 21, 1998, 5).

For some months now, we have witnessed an event which fills us with hope: the process of normalizing relations between two peoples following years of estrangement. It is a process, a sign of the victory of the culture of encounter and dialogue, "the system of universal growth" over "the forever-dead system of groups and dynasties," as José Martí said (*ibid.*). I urge political leaders to persevere on this path and to develop all its potentialities as a proof of the high service which they are called to carry out on behalf of the peace and well-being of their peoples, of all America, and as an example of reconciliation for the entire world. The world needs reconciliation in this climate of a piecemeal third world war in which we are living.

I place these days under the protection of Our Lady of Charity of El Cobre, Blessed Olallo Valdés and Blessed José López Pietreira, and Venerable Félix Varela, the great promoter of love between Cubans and all peoples, so that our bonds of peace, solidarity, and mutual respect may ever increase.

Once again, thank you, Mr. President.

II

The Call to Serve

Homily of Pope Francis
Mass, Plaza de la Revolución, Havana, Cuba
Sunday, September 20, 2015

Jesus asks his disciples an apparently indiscreet question: "What were you discussing along the way?" It is a question which he could also ask each of us today: "What do you talk about every day?" "What are your aspirations?" The Gospel tells us that the disciples "did not answer because on the way they had been arguing about who was the most important." They were ashamed to tell Jesus what they were talking about. Like the disciples then, today we too can be caught up in these same arguments: who is the most important?

Jesus does not press the question. He does not force them to tell him what they were talking about on the way. But the question lingers, not only in the minds of the disciples, but also in their hearts.

Who is the most important? This is a lifelong question to which, at different times, we must give an answer. We cannot escape the question; it is written on our hearts. I remember more than once, at family gatherings, children being asked: "Who do you love more, Mommy or Daddy?" It's like asking them: "Who is the most important for you?" But is this only a game we play with children? The history of humanity has been marked by the answer we give to this question.

Jesus is not afraid of people's questions; he is not afraid of our humanity or the different things we are looking for. On the contrary, he knows the depths of the human heart, and, as a good teacher, he is always ready to encourage and support us. As usual, he takes up our searching, our aspirations, and he gives them a new horizon. As usual, he somehow finds an answer which can pose a new challenge, setting aside the "right answers," the standard replies we are expected to give. As usual, Jesus sets before us the "logic" of love. A mindset, an approach to life, which is capable of being lived out by all, because it is meant for all.

Far from any kind of elitism, the horizon to which Jesus points us is not for those few privileged souls capable of attaining the heights of knowledge or different levels of spirituality. The horizon to which Jesus points us always has to do with daily life, also here on "our island," something which can season our daily lives with eternity.

Who is the most important? Jesus is straightforward in his reply: "Whoever wishes to be the first — the most important — among you must be the last of all, and the servant of all." Whoever wishes to be great must serve others, not be served by others.

This is the great paradox of Jesus. The disciples were arguing about who would have the highest place, who would be chosen for privileges — they were the disciples, those closest to Jesus, and they were arguing about that — who would be above the common law, the general norm, in order to stand out in the quest for superiority over others! Who would climb the ladder most quickly to take the jobs which carry certain benefits.

Jesus upsets their "logic," their mindset, simply by telling them that life is lived authentically in a concrete commitment to our neighbor. That is, by serving.

The call to serve involves something special, to which we must be attentive. Serving means caring for their vulnerability. Caring for the vulnerable of our families, our society, our people. Theirs are the suffering, fragile, and downcast faces which Jesus tells us specifically to look at and which he asks us to love. With a love which takes shape in our actions and decisions. With a love which finds expression in whatever tasks we, as citizens, are called to perform. It is people of flesh and blood, people with individual lives and stories, and with all their frailty, that Jesus asks us to protect, to care for and to serve. Being a Christian entails promoting the dignity of our brothers and sisters, fighting for it, living for it. That is why Christians are constantly called to set aside their own wishes and desires, their pursuit of power, before the concrete gaze of those who are most vulnerable.

There is a kind of "service" which serves others, yet we need to be careful not to be tempted by another kind of service, one which is "self-serving" with regard to others. There is a way to go about serving which is interested in only helping "my people," "our people." This service always leaves "your people" outside and gives rise to a process of exclusion.

All of us are called by virtue of our Christian vocation to that service which truly serves and to help one another not to be tempted by a "service" which is really "self-serving." All of us are asked, indeed urged, by Jesus to care for one another out of love. Without looking to one side or the other to see what our neighbor is doing or not doing. Jesus says: "Whoever would be first among you must be the last, and the servant of all." That person will be the first. Jesus does not say: "If your neighbor wants to be first, let him be the servant!" We have to be careful to avoid judgmental looks and renew our belief in the transforming look to which Jesus invites us.

This caring for others out of love is not about being servile. Rather, it means putting the question of our brothers and sisters at the center. Service always looks to their faces, touches their flesh, senses their closeness, and even, in some cases, "suffers" that closeness and tries to help them. Service is never ideological, for we do not serve ideas, we serve people.

God's holy and faithful people in Cuba is a people with a taste for celebrations, for friendship, for beautiful things. It is a people which marches with songs of praise. It is a people which has its wounds, like every other people, yet knows how to stand up with open arms, to keep walking in hope, because it has a vocation of grandeur. These were the seeds sown by your forebears. Today I ask you to care for this vocation of yours, to care for these gifts which God has given you, but above all I invite you to care for and be at the service of the frailty of your brothers and sisters. Do not neglect them for plans which can be seductive but are unconcerned about the face of the person beside you. We know, we are witnesses of the incomparable power of the Resurrection, which "everywhere calls forth the seeds of a new world" (cf. *Evangelii Gaudium*, 276, 278).

Let us not forget the Good News we have heard today: the importance of a people, a nation, and the importance of individuals, which is always based on how they seek to serve their vulnerable brothers and sisters. Here we encounter one of the fruits of a true humanity.

Because, dear brothers and sisters: "whoever does not live to serve, does not 'serve' to live."

III

Attentive to the Needs of Others

Angelus, Homily of Pope Francis
Plaza de la Revolución, Havana, Cuba
Sunday, September 20, 2015

I thank Cardinal Jaime Ortega y Alamino, archbishop of Havana, for his fraternal words, and I greet all my brother bishops, priests, religious, and lay faithful. I also greet the President and all the authorities present.

We have heard in the Gospel how the disciples were afraid to question Jesus when he spoke to them about his passion and death. He frightened them; they could not grasp the thought of seeing Jesus suffer on the cross. We too are tempted to flee from our own crosses and those of others, to withdraw from those who suffer. In concluding this Holy Mass, in which Jesus has once more given himself to us in his body and blood, let us now lift our gaze to the Virgin Mary, our Mother. We ask her to teach us to stand beside the cross of our brothers and sisters who suffer. To learn to see Jesus in every person bent low on the path of life, in all our brothers and sisters who hunger or thirst, who are naked or in prison or sick. With Mary our Mother, on the cross we can see who is truly "the greatest" and what it means to stand beside the Lord and to share in his glory.

Let us learn from Mary to keep our hearts awake and attentive to the needs of others. As the wedding feast of Cana teaches us, let us be concerned for the little details of life, and let us not tire of praying for one another, so that no one will lack the new wine of love, the joy which Jesus brings us.

At this time I feel bound to direct my thoughts to the beloved land of Colombia, "conscious of the crucial importance of the present moment when, with renewed effort and inspired by hope, its sons and daughters are seeking to build a peaceful society." May the blood shed by thousands of innocent people during long decades of armed conflict, united to that of the Lord Jesus Christ crucified, sustain all the efforts being made, also here on this beautiful island, to achieve definitive reconciliation. Thus may the long night of pain and violence, with the support of all Colombians, become an unending day of concord, justice, fraternity, and love, in respect for institutions and for national and international law, so that there may be lasting peace. Please, we do not have the right to allow ourselves yet another failure on this path of peace and reconciliation. Thank you, Mr. President, for all that you do in this work of reconciliation.

I ask you now to join in praying to Mary, that we may place all our concerns and hopes before the heart of Christ. We pray to her in a special way for those who have lost hope and find no reasons to keep fighting and for those who suffer from injustice, abandonment, and loneliness. We pray for the elderly, the infirm, children, and young people, for all families experiencing difficulty, that Mary may dry their tears, comfort them with a mother's love, and restore their hope and joy. Holy Mother, I commend to you these your sons and daughters in Cuba. May you never abandon them!

After the Final Blessing

And I ask you, please, not to forget to pray for me. Thank you.

IV

LEAVING EVERYTHING TO
FOLLOW JESUS

VESPERS WITH PRIESTS, MEN AND WOMEN RELIGIOUS,
AND SEMINARIANS
HOMILY OF POPE FRANCIS
CATHEDRAL, HAVANA, CUBA
SUNDAY, SEPTEMBER 20, 2015

~

Unprepared Remarks by the Holy Father
Cardinal Jaime Ortega y Alamino spoke to us about poverty and
Sister Yaileny (*Sister Yaileny Ponce Torres, D.C.*) spoke to us about
the little ones: "They are all children." I had prepared a homily to
give now, based on the biblical texts, but when prophets speak —
every priest is a prophet, all the baptized are prophets, every consecrated person is a prophet — then we should listen to them. So
I'm going to give the homily to Cardinal Jaime so that he can get
it to you and you can make it known. Later you can meditate on
it. And now let's talk a little about what these two prophets said.

Cardinal Jaime happened to say a very uncomfortable
word, an extremely uncomfortable word, one which goes against
the whole "cultural" structure of our world. He said "poverty,"
and he repeated it several times. I think the Lord wanted us to
keep hearing it and to receive it in our hearts. The spirit of the
world doesn't know this word, doesn't like it, hides it — not for
shame but for scorn. And if it has to sin and offend God in order
to avoid poverty, then that's what it does. The spirit of the world
does not love the way of the Son of God, who emptied himself,
became poor, became nothing, abased himself in order to be one
of us.

Poverty frightened that generous young man who had kept all the commandments, and so when Jesus told him, "Go, sell all that you have and give it to the poor," he was saddened. He was afraid of poverty. We are always trying to hide poverty, perhaps with good reason, but I'm talking about hiding it in our hearts. It is our duty to know how to administer our goods, for they are a gift from God. But when these goods enter your heart and begin to take over your life, that's where you can get lost. Then you are no longer like Jesus. Then you have your security where the sad young man had his, the one who went away sad.

For you, priests, consecrated men and women, I think what St. Ignatius said could be useful to you (and this is not just family propaganda here!). He said that poverty was the wall and the mother of consecrated life: the "mother" because it gives birth to greater confidence in God, and the "wall" because it protects us from all worldliness. How many ruined souls there are! Generous souls, like that of the sad young man, they started out well, then gradually became attached to the love of this wealthy worldliness and ended up badly. They ended up mediocre. They ended up without love because wealth impoverishes us, in a bad way. It takes away the best that we have, and strips us of the only wealth which is truly worthwhile, so that we put our security in something else.

The spirit of poverty, the spirit of detachment, the spirit of leaving everything behind in order to follow Jesus, this leaving everything is not something I am inventing. It appears frequently in the Gospel — in the calling of the first ones who left their boat, their nets, and followed him, those who left everything to follow Jesus.

A wise old priest once told me about what happens when the spirit of wealth, of wealthy worldliness enters the heart of a consecrated man or woman, a priest or bishop, or even a pope — anyone. He said that when we start to save up money to ensure our future — isn't this true? — then our future is not in Jesus but in a kind of spiritual insurance company which we manage. When, for example, a religious congregation begins to gather money and save, God is so good that he sends them a terrible bursar who brings them to bankruptcy. Such terrible bursars are some of the greatest blessings God grants his Church, because they make her free, they make her poor. Our Holy Mother the Church is poor; God wants her poor as he wanted our Holy Mother Mary to be poor.

So love poverty, like a mother. I would just suggest, should any of you want, that you ask yourself: "How is my spirit of poverty doing? How is my interior detachment?" I think this may be good for our consecrated life, our priestly life. After all, let us not forget that this is the first of the Beatitudes: "Blessed are the poor in spirit," those who are not attached to riches, to the powers of this world.

Sister also spoke to us of the least, of the little ones, who, whatever their age, we end up treating like children because they act like children. The least, the little ones. These are words that Jesus used, words that appear in the list of things on which we will be judged: "What you did to the least of these brothers and sisters, you did to me." There are pastoral services which may be more gratifying, from a human point of view, without being bad or worldly. But when we seek above all to prefer serving the little one, the outcast, the sick, those who are overlooked and unloved … when we serve these little ones, we serve Jesus in the best way possible.

So you were sent where you didn't want to go, and you cried. You cried because you didn't like it — which doesn't mean that you are a "whimpering nun," right? May God free us from whimpering nuns who are always complaining. This phrase isn't mine; St. Teresa of Avila said this to her nuns; it's her phrase. Woe to the nun who goes about all day moaning and groaning because she suffered an injustice. In the Castilian Spanish of that age, she said: "Woe to the nun who goes about saying, 'They treated me badly for no reason.'"

You cried because you were young, you had other dreams, perhaps you thought that in a school you could do more, that you could organize young people's futures. And they sent you there, to the "House of Mercy," where the tenderness and the mercy of God are most clearly shown, where the tenderness and the mercy of God become a caress. How many women and men religious "burn" — let me say it again, "burn" — their lives, caressing what is discarded, caressing those whom the world throws away, whom the world despises, whom the world wishes did not exist, those whom today's world, with new technologies, when it looks like they may come with a degenerative illness, thinks of "sending them back" before they are born. The little ones.

Young women full of dreams begin their consecrated lives by making God's tenderness, in his mercy, alive. At times they do not understand, they have no idea, but how wonderful it is for God, and how much good it does us, for example, when a person with palsy tries to smile or when they want to kiss you and they dribble on your face. That is the tenderness of God. That is the mercy of God. Or when they are upset and they hit you. "Burning" my life like this, with what the world would discard, that speaks to us of one person alone. It speaks to us of Jesus, who out of the sheer mercy of the Father became nothing. He "emptied himself," says the text of Philippians, Chapter Two. He became nothing. And these people to whom you dedicate your life imitate Jesus, not because they wanted to, but because this is the way they came into the world. They are nothing, they are kept out of sight, hidden; no one comes to see them. And if it is possible, and there's still time, they get "sent back."

So thank you for what you do, and, through you, I thank all those many women consecrated to the service of those considered "useless," since they cannot start a business, make money or do anything "constructive" at all — these brothers and sisters of ours, these little ones, the least among us. There Jesus shines forth! And that is where my decision for Jesus shines forth. I thank you and all the consecrated men and women who do this.

"Father, I'm not a nun. I don't take care of sick people. I'm a priest, and I have a parish, or I assist the pastor of a parish. Who is my beloved Jesus? Who is the little one? Who shows me most the mercy of the Father? Where must I find him or her?" Obviously I continue following the sequence of Matthew 25; there you have all of them: the hungry, the imprisoned, the sick — there you will meet them. But there is a special place for the priest, where the last, the least, and the littlest is found — and that is in the confessional. And there, when this man or this woman shows you their misery, take care, because it is the same misery as yours, the misery from which God saved you. Is that the case? When they reveal their misery to you, please don't give them a hard time. Don't scold them or punish them. If you are without sin, you can throw the first stone. But only then. Otherwise, think about your own sins; think that you could be that person. Think that you could potentially fall even lower, and think that in this moment you hold in your hands a treasure, which is the Father's mercy.

Please — I'm speaking to the priests — never tire of forgiving. Be forgivers. Like Jesus, never tire of forgiving. Don't hide behind fear or inflexibility. Just as this Sister — and all those in the same ministry as she is — do not become irate when they find a sick person who is dirty, but instead they serve him, clean him, take care of him. In the same way, when a penitent confesses, don't get upset or worked up, don't cast him out of the confessional, don't give them a hard time. Jesus embraced them. Jesus loved them. Tomorrow, we celebrate the feast of St. Matthew. He was a thief; he even, in a way, betrayed his own people. And the Gospel says that that evening Jesus went to have supper with him and others like him. St. Ambrose has a phrase which I find very moving: "Where there is mercy, the Spirit of Jesus is there; where there is rigor, his ministers alone are there."

Brother priest, brother bishop, do not be afraid of mercy. Let it flow through your hands and through your forgiving embrace, for the man or woman before you is one of the little ones. They are Jesus. This is what I thought I should say after hearing these two prophets. May the Lord give us these graces that these two have sown in our hearts: poverty and mercy. Because that is where Jesus is.

Homily

We are gathered in this historic Cathedral of Havana to sing with psalms the faithfulness of God towards his people, with thanksgiving for his presence and his infinite mercy. A faithfulness and mercy not only commemorated by this building but also by the living memory of some of the elderly among us, who know from experience that "his mercy endures forever and his faithfulness throughout the ages." For this, brothers and sisters, let us together give thanks.

Let us give thanks for the Spirit's presence in the rich and diverse charisms of all those missionaries who came to this land and became Cubans among Cubans, a sign that God's mercy is eternal.

The Gospel presents Jesus in dialogue with his Father. It brings us to the heart of the prayerful intimacy between the Father and the Son. As his hour drew near, Jesus prayed for his disciples, for those with him and for those who were yet to come (cf. John 17:20). We do well to remember that, in that crucial moment, Jesus made the lives of his disciples, our lives, a part of his prayer. He asked his Father to keep them united and joyful. Jesus knew full well the hearts of his disciples, and he knows full well our own. And so he prays to the Father to save them from a spirit of isolation, of finding refuge in their own certainties and comfort zones, of indifference to others and division into "cliques" which disfigure the richly diverse face of the Church. These are situations which lead to a kind of isolation and ennui, a sadness that slowly gives rise to resentment, to constant complaint, to boredom; this "is not God's will for us, nor is it the life in the Spirit" (*Evangelii Gaudium*, 2) to which he invited them, to which he has invited us. That is why Jesus prays that sadness and isolation will not prevail in our hearts. We want to do the same, we want to join in Jesus' prayer, in his words, so that we can say together: "Holy Father, keep them in thy name ... that they may be one, even as we are one" (John 17:11), "that your joy may be full" (John 15:11).

Jesus prays, and he invites us to pray, because he knows that some things can only be received as gifts; some things can only be experienced as gifts. Unity is a grace which can be bestowed upon us only by the Holy Spirit; we have to ask for this grace and do our best to be transformed by that gift.

Unity is often confused with uniformity — with actions, feelings, and words which are all identical. This is not unity; it is conformity. It kills the life of the Spirit; it kills the charisms which God has bestowed for the good of his people. Unity is threatened whenever we try to turn others into our own image and likeness. Unity is a gift, not something to be imposed by force or by decree. I am delighted to see you here, men and women of different generations, backgrounds, and experiences, all united by our common prayer. Let us ask God to increase our desire to be close to one another. To be neighbors, always there for one another, with all our many differences, interests, and ways of seeing things. To speak straightforwardly, despite our disagreements and disputes, and not behind one another's backs. May we be shepherds who are close to our people, open to their questions and problems. Conflicts and disagreements in the Church are to be expected and, I would even say, needed. They are a sign that the Church is alive and that the Spirit is still acting, still enlivening her. Woe to those communities without a "yes" and a "no"! They are like married couples who no longer argue, because they have lost interest, they have lost their love.

The Lord prays also that we may be filled with his own "complete joy" (cf. John 17:13). The joy of Christians, and especially of consecrated men and women, is a very clear sign of Christ's presence in their lives. When we see sad faces, it is a warning that something is wrong. Significantly, this is the request which Jesus makes of the Father just before he goes out to the Garden to renew his own "*fiat.*" I am certain that all of you have had to bear many sacrifices and, for some of you, for several decades now, these sacrifices have proved difficult. Jesus prays, at the moment of his own sacrifice, that we will never lose the joy of knowing that he overcomes the world. This certainty is what inspires us, morning after morning, to renew our faith. "With a tenderness which never disappoints but is always capable of restoring our joy" — by his prayer, and in the faces of our people — Christ "makes it possible for us to lift up our heads and to start anew" (*Evangelii Gaudium*, 3).

How important, how valuable for the life of the Cuban people, is this witness which always and everywhere radiates such joy, despite our weariness, our misgivings, and even our despair, that dangerous temptation which eats away at our soul!

Dear brothers and sisters, Jesus prays that all of us may be one and that his joy may abide within us. May we do likewise, as we unite ourselves to one another in prayer.

V

OPEN HEARTS AND OPEN MINDS

ADDRESS OF POPE FRANCIS TO STUDENTS AT
FATHER FÉLIX VARELA CULTURAL CENTER, HAVANA, CUBA
SUNDAY, SEPTEMBER 20, 2015

~

Unprepared Remarks of the Holy Father
You are standing up, and I am sitting. How rude! But you know why I am sitting; it is because I was taking notes on some of the things which our companion here was saying. Those are the things I want to talk about.

One really striking word he used was "dream." A Latin American writer once said that we all have two eyes: one of flesh and another of glass. With the eye of flesh, we see what is in front of us. With the eye of glass, we see what we dream of. Beautiful, isn't it?

In the daily reality of life, there has to be room for dreaming. A young person incapable of dreaming is cut off, self-enclosed. Everyone sometimes dreams of things which are never going to happen. But dream them anyway, desire them, seek new horizons, be open to great things.

I'm not sure if you use this word in Cuba, but in Argentina we say: "Don't be a pushover!" Don't bend or yield; open up. Open up and dream! Dream that with you the world can be different. Dream that if you give your best, you are going to help make this world a different place. Don't forget to dream! If you get carried away and dream too much, life will cut you short. It makes no difference; dream anyway, and share your dreams. Talk about the great things you wish for, because the greater your ability to dream, the farther you will have gone; even if life cuts you short halfway, you will still have gone a great distance. So, first of all, dream!

You said something which I had wrote down and under-lined. You said that we have to know how to welcome and accept those who think differently than we do. Honestly, sometimes we are very closed. We shut ourselves up in our little world: "Either things go my way or not at all." And you went even further. You said that we must not become enclosed in our little ideological or religious "worlds" ... that we need to outgrow forms of indi-vidualism.

When a religion becomes a "little world," it loses the best that it has; it stops worshiping God, believing in God. It be-comes a little world of words, of prayers, of "I am good and you are bad," of moral rules and regulations. When I have my ideol-ogy, my way of thinking, and you have yours, I lock myself up in this little world of ideology.

Open hearts and open minds. If you are different from me, then why don't we talk? Why do we always throw stones at one another over what separates us, what makes us different? Why don't we extend a hand where we have common ground? Why not try to speak about what we have in common, and then we can talk about where we differ. But I'm saying "talk"; I'm not saying "fight." I am not saying retreat into our "little worlds," to use your word. But this can only happen when I am able to speak about what I have in common with the other person, about things we can work on together.

In Buenos Aires, in a new parish in an extremely poor area, a group of university students were building some rooms for the parish. So the parish priest said to me: "Why don't you come one Saturday and I'll introduce them to you." They were building on Saturdays and Sundays. They were young men and women from the university. So I arrived, I saw them, and they were introduced to me: "This is the architect. He's Jewish. This one is Commu-nist. This one is a practicing Catholic." They were all different, yet they were all working for the common good.

This is called social friendship, where everyone works for the common good. Social enmity instead destroys. A family is destroyed by enmity. A country is destroyed by enmity. The world is destroyed by enmity. And the greatest enmity is war. Today we see that the world is being destroyed by war, because people are incapable of sitting down and talking. "Good, let's negotiate. What can we do together? Where are we going to draw the line? But let's not kill any more people." Where there is division, there is death: the death of the soul, since we are killing our ability to come together. We are killing social friendship. And this is what I'm asking you today: to find ways of building social friendship.

Then there was another word you said: "hope." The young are the hope of every people; we hear this all the time. But what is hope? Does it mean being optimistic? No. Optimism is a state of mind. Tomorrow, you wake up in a bad mood and you're not optimistic at all; you see everything in a bad light. Hope is something more. Hope involves suffering. Hope can accept suffering as part of building something; it is able to sacrifice. Are you able to sacrifice for the future, or do you simply want to live for the day and let those yet to come fend for themselves? Hope is fruitful. Hope gives life. Are you able to be life-giving? Or are you going to be young people who are spiritually barren, incapable of giving life to others, incapable of building social friendship, incapable of building a nation, incapable of doing great things?

Hope is fruitful. Hope comes from working, from having a job. Here I would mention a very grave problem in Europe: the number of young people who are unemployed. There are countries in Europe where forty percent of young people twenty-five years and younger are unemployed. I am thinking of one country. In another country, it is forty-seven percent and in another still, fifty percent.

Clearly, when a people is not concerned with providing work to its young — and when I say "a people," I don't mean governments; I mean the entire people who ought to be concerned whether these young people have jobs or not — that people has no future. Young people become part of the throwaway culture and all of us know that today, under the rule of mammon, things get thrown away and people get thrown away. Children are thrown away because they are not wanted, or killed before they are born. The elderly are thrown away — I'm speaking about the world in general — because they are no longer productive. In some countries, euthanasia is legal, but in so many others there is a hidden, covert euthanasia. Young people are thrown away because they are not given work. So then, what is left for a young person who has no work? When a country — a people — does not create employment opportunities for its young, what is left for these young people if not forms of addiction, or suicide, or going off in search of armies of destruction in order to make war?

This throwaway culture is harming us all; it is taking away our hope. And this is what you asked for in the name of young people: "We want hope." A hope which requires effort, hard work, and which bears fruit; a hope which gives us work and saves us from the throwaway culture. A hope which unites people, all people, because a people can join in looking to the future and in building social friendship — for all their differences — such a people has hope.

For me, meeting a young person without hope is, as I once said, like meeting a young retiree. There are young people who seem to have retired at the age of twenty-two. They are young people filled with existential dreariness, young people who have surrendered to defeatism, young people who whine and run away from life. The path of hope is not an easy one. And it can't be taken alone. There is an African proverb which says: "If you want to go quickly, walk alone, but if you want to go far, walk with another."

So this is what I have to say to you, the young people of Cuba. For all your different ways of thinking and seeing things, I would like you to walk with others, together, looking for hope, seeking the future and the nobility of your homeland.

We began with the word "dream," and I would like to conclude with another word that you said and which I myself often use: "the culture of encounter." Please, let us not "dis-encounter" one another. Let us go side-by-side with one other, as one. Encountering one another, even though we may think differently, even though we may feel differently. There is something bigger than we are, it is the grandeur of our people, the grandeur of our homeland, that beauty, that sweet hope for our homeland, which we must reach.

Thank you very much. I now leave you with my best wishes. For you I wish ... everything I told you; that is what I wish for you. I am going to pray for you. And I ask you to pray for me. And if any of you are not believers — and you can't pray because you don't believe — at least wish me well. May God bless you and bring you to tread this path of hope which leads to the culture of encounter, while avoiding those "little worlds" that our companion spoke about. May God bless all of you.

Dear Friends,

I am very happy to be with you here in this Cultural Center which is so important for Cuban history. I thank God for this opportunity to meet so many young people who, by their work, studies and training, are dreaming of, and already making real, the future of Cuba.

I thank Leonardo for his words of welcome, and particularly because, although he could have spoken about so many other important and concrete things such as our difficulties, fears, and doubts — as real and human as they are — he spoke to us about hope. He talked to us about those dreams and aspirations so firmly planted in the hearts of young Cubans, transcending all their differences in education, culture, beliefs, or ideas. Thank you, Leonardo, because, when I look at all of you, the first thing that comes into my mind and heart, too, is the word "hope." I cannot imagine a young person who is listless, without dreams or ideals, without a longing for something greater.

But what kind of hope does a young Cuban have at this moment of history? Nothing more or less than that of any other young person in any other part of the world, because hope speaks to us of something deeply rooted in every human heart, independently of our concrete circumstances and historical conditioning. Hope speaks to us of a thirst, an aspiration, a longing for a life of fulfillment, a desire to achieve great things, things which

fill our heart and lift our spirit to lofty realities like truth, goodness and beauty, justice and love. But it also involves taking risks.
It means being ready not to be seduced by what is fleeting, by
false promises of happiness, by immediate and selfish pleasures,
by a life of mediocrity and self-centeredness, which only fills the
heart with sadness and bitterness. No, hope is bold; it can look
beyond personal convenience, the petty securities and compen-
sations which limit our horizon, and can open us up to grand
ideals which make life more beautiful and worthwhile. I would
ask each one of you: "What is it that shapes your life? What lies
deep in your heart? Where do your hopes and aspirations lie? Are
you ready to put yourself on the line for the sake of something
even greater?"

Perhaps you may say: "Yes, Father, I am strongly attracted
to those ideals. I feel their call, their beauty, their light shining in
my heart. But I feel too weak; I am not ready to decide to take
the path of hope. The goal is lofty and my strength is all too little.
It is better to be content with small things, less grand but more
realistic, more within my reach." I can understand that reaction;
it is normal to feel weighed down by difficult and demanding
things. But take care not to yield to the temptation of a dis-
enchantment which paralyzes the intellect and the will, or that
apathy which is a radical form of pessimism about the future.
These attitudes end either in a flight from reality towards vain
utopias or else in selfish isolation and a cynicism deaf to the cry
for justice, truth, and humanity which rises up around us and
within us.

But what are we to do? How do we find paths of hope in
the situations in which we live? How do we make those hopes
for fulfillment, authenticity, justice, and truth become a reality
in our personal lives, in our country, and our world? I think that
there are three ideas which can help to keep our hope alive:

Hope is a path made of memory and discernment. Hope is
the virtue which goes places. It isn't simply a path we take for
the pleasure of it, but it has an end, a goal which is practical and
lights up our way. Hope is also nourished by memory; it looks
not only to the future but also to the past and present. To keep

moving forward in life, in addition to knowing where we want to go, we also need to know who we are and where we come from. Individuals or peoples who have no memory and erase their past risk losing their identity and destroying their future. So we need to remember who we are and in what our spiritual and moral heritage consists. This, I believe, was the experience and the insight of that great Cuban Father Félix Varela. Discernment is also needed, because it is essential to be open to reality and to be able to interpret it without fear or prejudice. Partial and ideological interpretations are useless; they only disfigure reality by trying to fit it into our preconceived schemas, and they always cause disappointment and despair. We need discernment and memory, because discernment is not blind; it is built on solid ethical and moral criteria which help us to see what is good and just.

Hope is a path taken with others. An African proverb says: "If you want to go fast, go alone; if you want to go far, go with others." Isolation and aloofness never generate hope, but closeness to others and encounter do. Left to ourselves, we will go nowhere. Nor by exclusion will we be able to build a future for anyone, even ourselves. A path of hope calls for a culture of encounter, dialogue, which can overcome conflict and sterile confrontation. To create that culture, it is vital to see different ways of thinking not in terms of risk but of richness and growth. The world needs this culture of encounter. It needs young people who seek to know and love one another, to journey together in building a country like that which José Martí dreamed of: "With all, and for the good of all."

Hope is a path of solidarity. The culture of encounter should naturally lead to a culture of solidarity. I was struck by what Leonardo said in his welcome, when he spoke of solidarity as a source of strength for overcoming all obstacles. Without solidarity, no country has a future. Beyond all other considerations or interests, there has to be concern for that person who may be my friend, my companion, but also someone who may think differently than I do, someone with his own ideas yet just as human and just as Cuban as I am. Simple tolerance is not enough; we have to go well beyond that, passing from a suspicious and defensive attitude to one of acceptance, cooperation, concrete service, and effective assistance. Do not be afraid of solidarity, service, and offering a helping hand, so that no one is excluded from the path.

This path of life is lit up by a higher hope: the hope born of our faith in Christ. He made himself our companion along the way. Not only does he encourage us, he also accompanies us; he is at our side and he extends a friendly hand to us. The Son of God, he wanted to become someone like us, to accompany us on our way. Faith in his presence, in his friendship and love, lights up all our hopes and dreams. With him at our side, we learn to discern what is real, to encounter and serve others, and to walk the path of solidarity.

Dear young people of Cuba, if God himself entered our history and became flesh in Jesus, if he shouldered our weakness and sin, then you need not be afraid of hope, or of the future, because God is on your side. He believes in you, and he hopes in you.

Dear friends, thank you for this meeting. May hope in Christ, your friend, always guide you along your path in life. And, please, remember to pray for me. May the Lord bless all of you.

VI

THE GAZE OF JESUS

MASS, HOMILY OF POPE FRANCIS ON THE FEAST OF
ST. MATTHEW
PLAZA DE LA REVOLUCIÓN, HOLGUÍN, CUBA
MONDAY, SEPTEMBER 21, 2015

We are celebrating the feast of the apostle and evangelist St. Matthew. We are celebrating the story of a conversion. Matthew himself, in his Gospel, tell us what it was like, this encounter which changed his life. He shows us an "exchange of glances" capable of changing history.

On a day like any other, as Matthew, the tax collector, was seated at his table, Jesus passed by, saw him, came up to him, and said, "Follow me." Matthew got up and followed him.

Jesus looked at him. How strong was the love in that look of Jesus, which moved Matthew to do what he did! What power must have been in his eyes to make Matthew get up from his table! We know that Matthew was a publican: he collected taxes from the Jews to give to the Romans. Publicans were looked down upon and considered sinners; for that reason they lived apart and were despised by others. One could hardly eat, speak, or pray with the likes of these. For the people, they were traitors: they extorted from their own to give to others. Publicans belonged to this social class.

Jesus stopped; he did not quickly turn away. He looked at Matthew calmly, peacefully. He looked at him with eyes of mercy; he looked at him as no one had ever looked at him before. And that look unlocked Matthew's heart; it set him free; it healed him; it gave him hope, a new life, as it did to Zacchaeus, to Bartimaeus, to Mary Magdalen, to Peter, and to each of us. Even if we dare not raise our eyes to the Lord, he always looks at us first. This is our story, and it is like that of so many others. Each of us can say: "I, too, am a sinner, whom Jesus has looked upon." I ask you today, in your homes or at church, when you are alone and at peace, to take a moment to recall with gratitude and happiness those situations, that moment, when the merciful gaze of God was felt in our lives.

Jesus' love goes before us, his look anticipates our needs. He can see beyond appearances, beyond sin, beyond failures and unworthiness. He sees beyond our rank in society. He sees beyond all of this. He sees our dignity as sons and daughters, a dignity at times sullied by sin, but one which endures in the depth of our soul. It is our dignity as sons and daughters. He came precisely to seek out all those who feel unworthy of God, unworthy of others. Let us allow Jesus to look at us. Let us allow his gaze to run over our streets. Let us allow that look to become our joy, our hope, our happiness in life.

After the Lord looked upon him with mercy, he said to Matthew: "Follow me." Matthew got up and followed him. After the look, a word. After love, the mission. Matthew is no longer the same; he is changed inside. The encounter with Jesus and his loving mercy transformed him. His table, his money, his exclusion, were all left behind. Before, he had sat waiting to collect his taxes, to take from others; now, with Jesus he must get up and give, give himself to others. Jesus looks at him and Matthew encounters the joy of service. For Matthew and for all who have felt the gaze of Jesus, other people are no longer to be "lived off," used and abused. The gaze of Jesus gives rise to missionary activity, service, self-giving. Other people are those whom Jesus serves. His love heals our short-sightedness and pushes us to look beyond, not to be satisfied with appearances or with what is politically correct.

Jesus goes before us, he precedes us; he opens the way and invites us to follow him. He invites us slowly to overcome our preconceptions and our reluctance to think that others, much less ourselves, can change. He challenges us daily with a question: "Do you believe? Do you believe it is possible that a tax collector can become a servant? Do you believe it is possible that a traitor can become a friend? Do you believe is possible that the son of a carpenter can be the Son of God?" His gaze transforms our way of seeing things; his heart transforms our hearts. God is a Father who seeks the salvation of each of his sons and daughters.

Let us gaze upon the Lord in prayer, in the Eucharist, in Confession, in our brothers and sisters, especially those who feel excluded or abandoned. May we learn to see them as Jesus sees us. Let us share his tenderness and mercy with the sick, prisoners, the elderly, and families in difficulty. Again and again we are called to learn from Jesus, who always sees what is most authentic in every person, which is the image of his Father.

I know the efforts and the sacrifices being made by the Church in Cuba to bring Christ's word and presence to all, even in the most remote areas. Here I would mention especially the "mission houses" which, given the shortage of churches and priests, provide for many people a place for prayer, for listening to the word of God, for catechesis and for community life. They are small signs of God's presence in our neighborhoods and a daily aid in our effort to respond to the plea of the apostle Paul: I "beg you to lead a life worthy of the calling to which you have been called, with all lowliness and meekness … forbearing one another in love, eager to maintain the unity of the Spirit in the bond of peace" (Ephesians 4:1-3).

I now turn my eyes to the Virgin Mary, Our Lady of Charity of El Cobre, whom Cuba embraced and to whom it opened its doors forever. I ask her to look with maternal love on all her children in this noble country. May her "eyes of mercy" ever keep watch over each of you, your homes, your families, and all those who feel that they have no place. In her love, may she protect us all as she once cared for Jesus. And may she teach us to look upon others in the same way that Jesus looked upon each one of us.

VII

Our Lady of Charity of El Cobre

Prayer of Pope Francis to the Virgen de la Caridad
Shrine of the Virgen de la Caridad del Cobre
Santiago, Cuba
Monday, September 21, 2015

Our Lady of Charity of El Cobre,
Patroness of Cuba!
Hail, Mary,
full of grace!
You are the beloved Daughter of the Father,
Mother of Christ, our God,
the living Temple
of the Holy Spirit.

You carry in your name,
Virgin of Charity,
the memory of God who is Love,
the memory of the new commandments of Jesus,
the evocation of the Holy Spirit:
love poured into our hearts,
the fire of charity
sent on Pentecost
upon the Church,
the gift of the full freedom
of the children of God.

Blessed are you among women
and blessed is the fruit
of your womb, Jesus!
You came to visit our people
And you chose to remain with us
As Mother and Lady of Cuba,
on our pilgrimage
through the paths of history.

Your name and your image
are carved
into the hearts and minds
of all Cubans,
both in the Country and abroad,
as a sign of hope
and the center of brotherly communion.
Holy Mary, Mother of God
and our Mother!

Pray for us
before your Son Jesus Christ,
intercede for us
with your motherly heart,
flooded with the love of the Holy Spirit.
Increase our faith,
awaken our hope,
broaden and strengthen our love.

Watch over our families,
protect our young people and our children,
console those who suffer.
Be the mother of the faithful
and of the pastors of the Church,
model and star of the new evangelization.

Mother of reconciliation!
Gather your people
scattered around the earth.
Make of our Cuban nation

a house of brothers and sisters
that this people may open wide
her mind, her heart
and her life to Christ,
the one Savior and Redeemer,
who lives and reigns with the Father
and the Holy Spirit
forever and ever.

Amen.

VIII

Mary and the Revolution of Tenderness

Mass, Homily of Pope Francis
Minor Basilica of the Shrine "Virgen de la Caridad
del Cobre," Santiago, Cuba
Tuesday, September 22, 2015

The Gospel we have just heard tells us about something the Lord does every time he visits us: he calls us out of our house. These are images which we are asked to contemplate over and over again. God's presence in our lives never leaves us tranquil: it always pushes to do something. When God comes, he always calls us out of our house. We are visited so that we can visit others; we are encountered so as to encounter others; we receive love in order to give love.

In the Gospel we see Mary, the first disciple. A young woman of perhaps between fifteen and seventeen years of age who, in a small village of Palestine, was visited by the Lord, who told her that she was to be the mother of the Savior. Mary was far from "thinking it was all about her," or thinking that everyone had to come and wait upon her; she left her house and went out to serve. First she goes to help her cousin Elizabeth. The joy which blossoms when we know that God is with us, with our people, gets our hearts beating, gets our legs moving, and "draws us out of ourselves." It leads us to take the joy we have received and to share it in service, in those "pregnant" situations which our neighbors or families may be experiencing.

The Gospel tells us that Mary went in haste, slowly but surely, with a steady pace, neither too fast nor so slow as never to get there. Neither anxious nor distracted, Mary goes with haste to accompany her cousin who conceived in her old age. Henceforth this was always to be her way. She has always been the woman who visits men and women, children, the elderly, and the young. She has visited and accompanied many of our peoples in the drama of their birth; she has watched over the struggles of those who fought to defend the rights of their children. And now, she continues to bring us the Word of Life, her Son, Our Lord.

These lands have also been visited by her maternal presence. The Cuban homeland was born and grew, warmed by devotion to Our Lady of Charity. As the bishops of this country have written: "In a special and unique way, she has molded the Cuban soul, inspiring the highest ideals of love of God, the family, and the nation in the heart of the Cuban people."

This was what your fellow citizens also stated a hundred years ago, when they asked Pope Benedict XV to declare Our Lady of Charity the Patroness of Cuba. They wrote that "neither disgrace nor poverty were ever able to crush the faith and the love which our Catholic people profess for the Virgin of Charity, for whom, in all their trials, when death was imminent or desperation was at the door, there arose, like a light scattering the darkness of every peril, like a comforting dew ... the vision of that Blessed Virgin, utterly Cuban and loved as such by our cherished mothers, blessed as such by our wives." Thus they wrote one hundred years ago.

In this shrine, which keeps alive the memory of God's holy and faithful pilgrim people in Cuba, Mary is venerated as the Mother of Charity. From here she protects our roots, our identity, so that we may never stray to paths of despair. The soul of the Cuban people, as we have just heard, was forged amid suffering and privation which could not suppress the faith, that faith which was kept alive thanks to all those grandmothers who fostered, in the daily life of their homes, the living presence of God, the presence of the Father who liberates, strengthens, heals, grants courage, and serves as a sure refuge and the sign of a new resurrection. Grandmothers, mothers, and so many others who with tenderness and love were signs of visitation, like Mary, of valor and faith for their grandchildren, in their families, they kept open a tiny space, small as a mustard seed, through which the Holy Spirit continued to accompany the heartbeat of this people.

"Whenever we look to Mary, we come to believe once again in the revolutionary nature of love and tenderness" (*Evangelii Gaudium*, 288).

Generation after generation, day after day, we are asked to renew our faith. We are asked to live the revolution of tenderness as Mary, our Mother of Charity, did. We are invited to "leave home" and to open our eyes and hearts to others. Our revolution comes about through tenderness, through the joy which always becomes closeness and compassion — which is not pity, but suffering with, so as to free — and leads us to get involved in, and to serve, the life of others. Our faith makes us leave our homes and go forth to encounter others, to share their joys, their hopes, and their frustrations. Our faith "calls us out of our house," to visit the sick, the prisoner and those who mourn. It makes us able to laugh with those who laugh, and rejoice with our neighbors who rejoice.

Like Mary, we want to be a Church which serves, which leaves home and goes forth, which goes forth from its chapels, forth from its sacristies, in order to accompany life, to sustain hope, to be the sign of unity of a noble and worthy people. Like Mary, Mother of Charity, we want to be a Church which goes forth to build bridges, to break down walls, to sow seeds of reconciliation. Like Mary, we want to be a Church which can accompany all those "pregnant" situations of our people, committed to life, to culture, to society, not washing our hands but rather walking together with our brothers and sisters. Together, serving and helping. All children of God, children of Mary, children of this noble Cuban land.

This is our most valuable treasure (*cobre*), this is our greatest wealth and the best legacy we can give: to learn like Mary to leave home and set out on the path of visitation. And to learn to pray with Mary, for her prayer is one of remembrance and gratitude; it is the canticle of the People of God on their pilgrimage through history. It is the living reminder that God passes through our midst; the perennial memory that God has looked upon the lowliness of his people, he has come to the aid of his servant, even as promised to our forebears and their children for ever.

IX

THE WARMTH OF FAMILY LIFE

MEETING WITH FAMILIES
ADDRESS OF POPE FRANCIS
CATHEDRAL OF OUR LADY OF THE ASSUMPTION,
SANTIAGO, CUBA
TUESDAY, SEPTEMBER 22, 2015

~

We are here as a family! And whenever we come together as a family, we feel at home. Thank you, Cuban families. Thank you, Cubans, for making me feel part of a family, for making me feel at home, in these days. Thank you for everything. This meeting is like "the icing on the cake." To conclude my visit with this family gathering is a reason to thank God for the "warmth" spread by people who know how to welcome and accept someone, to make him feel at home. Thank you to all Cubans!

I am grateful to Archbishop Dionisio García of Santiago for his greetings in the name of all present, and to the married couple who were not afraid to share with all of us their hopes and struggles in trying to make their home a "domestic church."

John's Gospel tells us that Jesus worked his first miracle at the wedding feast of Cana, at a family party. There he was, with Mary, his mother, and some of his disciples. They were sharing in a family celebration.

Weddings are special times in many people's lives. For the "older folks," parents and grandparents, it is an opportunity to reap the fruits of what they have sown. Our hearts rejoice when we see children grow up and make a home of their own. For a moment, we see that everything we worked for was worth the effort. To raise children, to support and encourage them, to help them want to make a life for themselves and form a family: this is a great challenge for parents. Weddings, too, show us the joy of young spouses. The future is open before them, and everything has the flavor of a new home, of hope. Weddings always bring together the past which we inherit and the future in which we put our hope. There is memory and hope. Weddings are an opportunity to be grateful for everything which has brought us to this day, with the same love which we have received.

Jesus begins his public life at a wedding. He enters into that history of sowing and reaping, of dreams and quests, of efforts and commitments, of hard work which tills the land so that it can yield fruit. Jesus began his life within a family, within a home. And it is precisely our homes into which he continues to enter, and of which he becomes a part. He likes to be part of a family.

It is interesting to see how Jesus also shows up at meals, at dinners. Eating with different people, visiting different homes, was a special way for him to make known God's plan. He goes to the home of his friends, Martha and Mary, but he is not choosy; it makes no difference to him whether publicans or sinners are there, like Zacchaeus. He goes to Zacchaeus' house. He didn't just act this way himself; when he sent his disciples out to proclaim the good news of the kingdom of God he told them: stay in the same house, eating and drinking what they provide (Luke 10:7). Weddings, visits to people's homes, dinners: those moments in people's lives become "special" because Jesus chose to be part of them.

I remember in my former diocese how many families told me that almost the only time they came together was at dinner, in the evening after work, when the children had finished their homework. These were special times in the life of the family. They talked about what happened that day and what each of them had done; they tidied the house, put things away and organized their chores for the next few days; the children bickered; but it was a special time. These were also times when someone might come home tired, or when arguments or disagreements might break out between husband and wife, but there are worse things to fear. I am more afraid of marriages where spouses tell me they have never, ever argued. It is rare. Jesus chooses all those times to show us the love of God. He chooses those moments to enter into our hearts and to help us to discover the Spirit of life at work in our homes and our daily affairs.

It is in the home that we learn fraternity and solidarity, we learn not to be overbearing. It is in the home that we learn to receive, to appreciate life as a blessing and to realize that we need one another to move forward. It is in the home that we experience forgiveness, and we are constantly invited to forgive and to grow. It is interesting that in the home there is no room for "putting on masks": we are who we are, and in one way or another we are called to do our best for others.

That is why the Christian community calls families "domestic churches." It is in the warmth of the home that faith fills every corner, lights up every space, builds community. At those moments, people learn to discover God's love present and at work.

In many cultures today, these spaces are shrinking, these experiences of family are disappearing, and everything is slowly breaking up, growing apart. We have fewer moments in common, to stay together, to stay at home as a family. As a result, we don't know how to be patient, we don't know how to ask permission, we don't know how to beg forgiveness, we don't know how to say "thank you," because our homes are growing empty. Not of people, but empty of relationships, empty of human contact, empty of encounters, between parents, children, grandparents, grandchildren, and siblings. Not long ago, someone who works with me told me that his wife and children had gone off on vacation, while he remained home alone because he had to work those days. The first day, the house was completely quiet, "at peace"; he was happy and nothing was out of place. On the third day, when I asked him how things were going, he told me: I wish they would all come back soon. He felt he couldn't live without his wife and children. And that is beautiful, very beautiful.

Without family, without the warmth of home, life grows empty, there is a weakening of the networks which sustain us in adversity, the networks which nurture us in daily living and motivate us to build a better future. The family saves us from two present-day phenomena, two things which happen every day: fragmentation, that is, division, and uniformity. In both cases, people turn into isolated individuals, easy to manipulate and to rule. Then in our world we see societies which are divided, broken, separated or rigidly uniform. These are a result of the breakup of family bonds, the loss of those relationships which make us who we are, which teach us to be persons. Then we forget how to say dad, mom, son, daughter, grandfather, grandmother ... we gradually lose a sense of these basic relationships, relationships at the basis of the name we bear.

The family is a school of humanity, a school which teaches us to open our hearts to others' needs, to be attentive to their lives. When we live together life as a family, we keep our little ways of being selfish in check — they will always be there, because each of us has a touch of selfishness — but when there is no family life, what results are those "me, myself and I" personalities who are completely self-centered and lacking any sense of solidarity, fraternity, cooperation, love and fraternal disagreements. They don't have it. Amid all the difficulties troubling our families in our world today, please, never forget one thing: families are not a problem. They are first and foremost an opportunity, an opportunity which we have to care for, protect and support. In other words, they are a blessing. Once you begin to see the family as a problem, you get bogged down, you don't move forward, because you are caught up in yourself.

Nowadays we talk a lot about the future, about the kind of world we want to leave to our children, the kind of society we want for them. I believe that one possible answer lies in looking at ourselves, at this family which spoke to us. Let us leave behind a world with families. No doubt about it: the perfect family does not exist; there are no perfect husbands and wives, perfect parents, perfect children or — if they will not get mad at me for saying this, perfect mothers-in-law. Those families don't exist. But that does not prevent families from being the answer for the future. God inspires us to love, and love always engages with the persons it loves. Love always engages with the persons it loves. So let us care for our families, true schools for the future. Let us care for our families, true spaces of freedom. Let us care for families, true centers of humanity.

Here an image comes to mind: when I greet people during my Wednesday audiences, many women show me that they are pregnant and ask me to bless them. I am going to propose something to all those women who are "pregnant with hope," because a child is a hope. Right now, put your hands over your baby. Whether you are here, or following by radio or television, do it now. And to each of you, and to each baby boy or girl you are expecting, I give my blessing. So all of you, as you put your hands over your baby, I give you my blessing: in the name of the Father, and of the Son, and of the Holy Spirit. And I pray that your child will be born healthy and grow up well, that you can be good parents. Caress the child you are expecting.

I do not want to end without mentioning the Eucharist. All of you know very well that Jesus chose a meal to be the setting for his memorial. He chose a specific moment of family life as the "place" of his presence among us. A moment which we have all experienced, a moment we all understand: a meal.

The Eucharist is the meal of Jesus' family, which the world over gathers to hear his word and to be fed by his body. Jesus is the Bread of Life for our families. He wants to be ever present, nourishing us by his love, sustaining us in faith, helping us to walk in hope, so that in every situation we can experience the true Bread of Heaven.

In a few days I will join families from across the globe in the World Meeting of Families and, in less than a month, in the Synod of Bishops devoted to the family. I ask you to pray. I ask you to pray in particular for these two events, so that together we can find ways to help one another and to care for the family, so that we can continue to discover Emmanuel, the God who dwells in the midst of his people, and makes each family, and all families, his home. I am counting on your prayers. Thank you.

Final Greeting of the Holy Father from the Terrace

Thank you for your warm welcome, thank you! Cubans really are kind and gracious; you make people feel at home. Many thanks. I want to speak a word of hope, a word of hope that can perhaps make us look both backwards and ahead. Looking back, memory. Memory of all those who brought us to life, and especially grandparents. A special greeting to grandparents. We forget about the elderly. The elderly are our living memory. Then, looking ahead, the children and the young who are the strength of a people. A people which cares for its elderly and cares for its children and young people will surely triumph. God bless you and let me give you my blessing, but on one condition; you are going to have to pay a price. I would ask you to pray for me. That is the condition. May almighty God bless you, the Father, and the Son, and the Holy Spirit. Goodbye, and thank you.

X

IN-FLIGHT PRESS CONFERENCE

PAPAL FLIGHT
PRESS CONFERENCE OF POPE FRANCIS FROM SANTIAGO DE
CUBA TO WASHINGTON, D.C.
TUESDAY, SEPTEMBER 22, 2015

~

Father Feerico Lombardi
Holy Father, thank you for being here with us on this connecting flight: in this way we can have a conversation with you to reflect a little on this first stage of your journey, to Cuba, which was very beautiful and demanding.

We have a list of several colleagues who have prepared a few questions. The questions will be asked in Spanish or Italian, and they would ask you to respond in Spanish to our Cuban friend, who will ask the first question. Others have asked if they can use Italian, because in general they understand it better.… This time we won't worry about Guaranì…!

The first question is asked by our friend Rosa Miriam Elizalde from "Cubadebate."

Rosa Miriam Elizalde
Thank you. Your Holiness, it was really an honor and a pleasure to accompany you on this journey, and also a great joy. I think my question is fairly obvious: I would like to know your thoughts about the United States embargo of Cuba, and if you will speak about this before the United States Congress.

Pope Francis
The issue of the embargo is under negotiation. That is public: both Presidents have spoken about it. So it is something public

which has to do with their efforts to build better relations. My hope is that things prove successful, that an agreement satisfactory to both parties can be reached. As for the position of the Holy See with regard to embargos, previous popes have spoken of this, not just in this case, but also in other cases. There is the Church's social doctrine on the question and I would refer to that; it is clear and just. As for the United States Congress, I have prepared my address, but I am not supposed to say that! But I am thinking about what I will say on the matter. Not specifically on this issue; rather, more generally on the issue of bilateral or multilateral agreements, as signposts on the way towards coexistence. But this specific matter — as I recall, and without wanting to say something wrong, it is not mentioned, almost certainly not.

Father Lombardi
Now another Rosa. We are beginning with two ladies called Rosa; this is a good sign. Rosa Flores of CNN. Could you speak in Italian please? Or in Spanish…. The pope will respond in Italian.

Rosa Flores
Holy Father, good evening. I am Rosa Flores of CNN. We heard that more than fifty dissidents were arrested outside the Nunciature because they were trying to meet with you. The first question is: Would you want to meet the dissidents? And then, should such a meeting take place, what would you say to them?

Pope Francis
First, I didn't hear that this happened. I didn't hear any news. Someone can say: yes, no, I don't know…. Directly, I don't know. Your two questions have to do with "What if's …" Would I like it if …? What would happen if …? I like to meet everyone. Because first and foremost I think every person is a child of God, with rights. Second, because meeting another person is enriching. Yes, I would like to meet with them. If you want me to keep speaking about dissidents, I can say something very concrete. First of all, the Nunciature made it very clear that I was not going to grant audiences, because audiences were being sought not only by dissidents but also by other groups, including some heads of other

states. I am visiting one country, and one alone. No audience was planned either with dissidents or others. Secondly, phone calls were made from the nunciature to certain people belonging to this group of dissidents.... The nuncio's job was to tell them that, when I arrived at the cathedral for the meeting with the consecrated persons, I would be happy to greet those who were there. A greeting. Yes, that is right. But since no one spoke up in the greeting, I don't know if they were there or not. I greeted those who were there. Above all, I greeted the sick, the people in wheelchairs. But no one identified himself or herself as a dissident. Several calls were made from the nunciature to invite them for a passing greeting.

Flores
But what would you say to them?

Pope Francis
I don't know what I would say to them. I wish everyone well, but what one says comes at that moment, so I don't know.

Father Lombardi
Now we have Silvia Poggioli of National Public Radio, a major network in the United States.

Silvia Poggioli
Sorry, I would like to ask you: In the decades when Fidel Castro was in power, the Catholic Church in Cuba suffered greatly. In your meeting with Fidel, did you have the sense that he had any regrets?

Pope Francis
Regret is something very personal, a matter of conscience. In the meeting with Fidel, I talked about some Jesuits we knew, because one of the gifts I brought him was a book by Father Llorente, a good friend of his, a Jesuit, and a compact disc of Father Llorente's talks; I also gave him two books by Father Pronzato which he will surely appreciate. We talked about those things. We also talked a lot about the encyclical *Laudato Si'*, because he is very interested in ecology. It was less a formal meeting than a sponta-

neous one. His family was there, as were my entourage and my driver; but we were somewhat apart, he, his wife and I, and the others could not hear, but they were there. That is what we spoke about. Lots about the encyclical, because this is a concern of his. We did not talk about the past. Except for the Jesuit school, what the Jesuits were like, how they made him work … all that we did talk about.

Father Lombardi
Now it is the turn of Gian Guido Vecchi, whom I believe you know from Corriere della Sera.

Gian Guido Vecchi
Holiness, your reflections on, and criticism of, the inequality of the world economic system, the danger of our destroying the planet, the arms trade, are also uncomfortable, in the sense that they touch on powerful interests. On the eve of this trip, there was some pretty bizarre talk — reported even in important media worldwide — about sectors of American society which were starting to wonder if the pope was Catholic.… There had already been talk about a "communist pope"; now they are asking: "Is the pope Catholic?" What do you have to say about this?

Pope Francis
A friend of mine, a cardinal, told me about a lady who came to him very concerned, a good Catholic lady, a bit rigid but very good, and asked him if it was true that the Bible talked about an antichrist. He explained that it is found in the Book of Revelation. Then she asked if it spoke of an antipope! "Why do you ask?" he said. "Because I am sure that Pope Francis is the antipope!" "And where did you get that idea?" "Because he doesn't wear red shoes!" There it is, as it happened. The reasons for thinking that someone is a communist or not.… I am sure that I haven't said anything more than what is contained in the Church's social teaching. On the other flight [returning from Latin America], one of your colleagues — I don't know if she is here — said, after I went to speak to the popular movements, "You held out a hand to this popular movement" — something more or less like that

— "but will the Church follow you?" And my reply was: "I'm the one who follows the Church." I do not believe I was wrong there. I don't believe that I have said anything not found in the Church's social teaching. Things can be explained, and maybe an explanation could give the impression of being a little more "leftist," but that would be an error of explanation. No, my teaching, on all of this, in *Laudato Si'*, on economic imperialism and all these things, is that of the Church's social teaching. And if I need to recite the Creed, I am ready to do it!

Father Lombardi
Now it is the turn of Jean-Louis de la Vaissiere, from "France Presse."

Jean-Louis de la Vaissiere
Good evening, Holy Father. Thank you for this visit; always interesting. In your last visit to Latin America, you sharply criticized the liberal capitalist system. In Cuba, it seems that your critiques of the communist system were less severe, more "soft." Why these differences?

Pope Francis
In my speeches in Cuba, I always mentioned the Church's social teaching. I spoke clearly, not gingerly or gently, about the things that need to be corrected. But also, as far as the first part of the question goes, I didn't say anything harsher than what I wrote in the encyclical, and also in *Evangelii Gaudium*, on unfettered or liberal capitalism: it is all there. I don't recall having said anything more than that. I don't know, if you remember, help me to recall … I said what I had written, and that is more than enough! Then too, just as I said to your colleague: all this is part of the Church's social doctrine. But here in Cuba — and this perhaps will help to answer your question — the visit was a very pastoral visit with the Catholic community, with Christians, but also with people of goodwill, and for this reason my interventions were homilies.… Also with the young people — who were young believers and nonbelievers, and among the believers members of different religions — it was all about hope and encouragement to dialogue

among themselves, to walk together, to seek the things which unite us and not those which divide us, to build bridges.... It was a more pastoral language, whereas the encyclical had to discuss technical matters and the things which you brought up. But if you can remember something that I said during the other visit which was harsh, let me know, because really, I don't remember.

Father Lombardi
Now we hear from an old friend, Nelson Castro, from "Radio Continental" in Argentina.

Pope Francis
... who is a good doctor ...

Nelson Castro
Good evening, Holy Father. My question goes back to the topic of dissidents. Two things. Why the decision not to receive the dissidents, and secondly, one of them did approach you but was taken away and arrested.... The question is whether the Catholic Church will play a role in seeking an opening to political liberties, given the role it played in the re-establishment of relations between Cuba and the United States? The issue of liberties, which is a problem for those who think differently in Cuba. Does the Holy See foresee a role for the Catholic Church in Cuba's future?

Pope Francis
First, about not receiving "them." I did not receive anyone in private audience. That goes for everyone. There was also a head of state who asked.... No, it didn't have anything to do with the dissidents. I have already explained how the dissidents were treated. The Church in Cuba drew up a list of prisoners for grants of amnesty. Amnesty was granted to about three thousand five hundred people ... the figure was given me by the president of the episcopal conference.... Yes, more than three thousand. And there are other cases under study. The Church in Cuba is working for grants of amnesty. For example, someone said to me that it would be nice to put an end to life sentences, lifetime imprisonment. To my mind, life imprisonment is a kind of concealed

death penalty. I said this publicly in an address to European jurists. You are there, dying daily without the hope of ever being freed. This is one hypothesis; another is that they could issue amnesties every one or two years. But the Church is working, has worked … I am not saying that these more than three thousand people have been freed on the basis of the Church's lists. The Church did make a list — I don't know of how many persons — and asked officially for grants of amnesty and it will continue to do so.

Father Lombardi
The last on our list for this conference is Rogelio Mora of Telemundo.

Rogelio Mora
Holy Father, a doctor visits someone who is sick, not someone who is healthy. In less than twenty years, three popes have visited Cuba. Does this mean that Cuba is sick?

Pope Francis
I didn't understand the question.

Mora
Can the fact that three popes have visited Cuba in less than twenty years be interpreted to mean that there is a sickness on the island, that the island is suffering from something.…

Pope Francis
Now I see what you mean. No, no. The first to visit was John Paul II, the historic first visit. But that was normal: he visited any number of countries, including countries hostile to the Church. The second was Pope Benedict, but that was also normal. My own visit was somewhat by chance, because I had thought of entering the United States from Mexico. Initially the idea was to enter from Ciudad Juárez, on the border with Mexico. But to go to Mexico without going to Our Lady of Guadalupe would have been an insult! So that didn't happen. Then last December 17, after the process which had been quietly going on for almost a year became public, I thought: I would like to enter the United States

from Cuba. I chose to for that reason. Not because Cuba has a particular illness that other countries don't have. So I wouldn't interpret the three visits that way. There are various countries which the two most recent popes visited, and I have also visited, like Brazil. And John Paul II visited Brazil three or four times, and it didn't have any particular illness. I am happy to have met the Cuban people, the Christian communities of Cuba. Today's meeting with families was very nice, it was very beautiful.

I thank you for the work you still have to do, which will be demanding, because three cities.... There were twenty-four speeches, and in Cuba I gave eight.... Thank you very much for your work. And pray for me!

Father Lombardi
Many thanks indeed, Your Holiness. And good wishes, because, if we have work to do, you have even more. So we offer you our best wishes and we will continue to help you as communicators, so that your words can truly serve all of humanity and contribute to peace, as you said at the beginning. Thank you.

XI

FREEDOM, RELIGIOUS LIBERTY, AND CARE FOR OUR COMMON HOME

WELCOMING CEREMONY
ADDRESS OF POPE FRANCIS
SOUTH LAWN OF THE WHITE HOUSE, WASHINGTON, D.C.
WEDNESDAY, SEPTEMBER 23, 2015

~

Good morning!

Mr. President,

I am deeply grateful for your welcome in the name of all Americans. As the son of an immigrant family, I am happy to be a guest in this country, which was largely built by such families. I look forward to these days of encounter and dialogue, in which I hope to listen to, and share, many of the hopes and dreams of the American people.

During my visit I will have the honor of addressing Congress, where I hope, as a brother of this country, to offer words of encouragement to those called to guide the nation's political future in fidelity to its founding principles. I will also travel to Philadelphia for the Eighth World Meeting of Families, to celebrate and support the institutions of marriage and the family at this, a critical moment in the history of our civilization.

Mr. President, together with their fellow citizens, American Catholics are committed to building a society which is truly tolerant and inclusive, to safeguarding the rights of individuals and communities, and to rejecting every form of unjust discrimination. With countless other people of good will, they are likewise concerned that efforts to build a just and wisely ordered society respect their deepest concerns and their right to religious liberty. That freedom remains one of America's most precious possessions. And, as my brothers, the United States Bishops, have reminded us, all are called to be vigilant, precisely as good citizens, to preserve and defend that freedom from everything that would threaten or compromise it.

Mr. President, I find it encouraging that you are proposing an initiative for reducing air pollution. Accepting the urgency, it seems clear to me also that climate change is a problem which can no longer be left to a future generation. When it comes to the care of our "common home," we are living at a critical moment of history. We still have time to make the changes needed to bring about "a sustainable and integral development, for we know that things can change" (*Laudato Si'*, 13). Such change demands on our part a serious and responsible recognition not only of the kind of world we may be leaving to our children, but also to the millions of people living under a system which has overlooked them. Our common home has been part of this group of the excluded which cries out to heaven and which today powerfully strikes our homes, our cities, and our societies. To use a telling phrase of the Reverend Martin Luther King, we can say that we have defaulted on a promissory note and now is the time to honor it.

We know by faith that "the Creator does not abandon us; he never forsakes his loving plan or repents of having created us. Humanity still has the ability to work together in building our common home" (*Laudato Si'*, 13). As Christians inspired by this certainty, we wish to commit ourselves to the conscious and responsible care of our common home.

Mr. President, the efforts which were recently made to mend broken relationships and to open new doors to cooperation within our human family represent positive steps along the path of reconciliation, justice and freedom. I would like all men and women of good will in this great nation to support the efforts of the international community to protect the vulnerable in our world and to stimulate integral and inclusive models of development, so that our brothers and sisters everywhere may know the blessings of peace and prosperity which God wills for all his children.

Mr. President, once again I thank you for your welcome, and I look forward to these days in your country. God bless America!

XII

Undivided Hearts, Selfless Devotion

Meeting with Bishops of the United States of America
Address of Pope Francis
Cathedral of St. Matthew, Washington, D.C.
Wednesday, September 23, 2015

Dear Brother Bishops,

First of all, I wish to send a greeting to the Jewish community, our Jewish brothers and sisters, who today are celebrating Yom Kippur. May the Lord bless them with peace and help them to advance on the path of holiness, as we heard today in his word: "You shall be holy; for I ... am holy" (Leviticus 19:2).

I am pleased that we can meet at this point in the apostolic mission which has brought me to your country. I thank Cardinal [Donald] Wuerl and Archbishop [Joseph] Kurtz for their kind words in your name. I am very appreciative of your welcome and the generous efforts made to help plan and organize my stay.

As I look out with affection at you, their pastors, I would like to embrace all the local Churches over which you exercise loving responsibility. I would ask you to share my affection and spiritual closeness with the People of God throughout this vast land.

The heart of the pope expands to include everyone. To testify to the immensity of God's love is the heart of the mission entrusted to the Successor of Peter, the Vicar of the One who on the cross embraced the whole of mankind. May no member of

Christ's Body and the American people feel excluded from the pope's embrace. Wherever the name of Jesus is spoken, may the pope's voice also be heard to affirm that: *"He is the Savior!"* From your great coastal cities to the plains of the Midwest, from the deep South to the far reaches of the West, wherever your people gather in the Eucharistic assembly, may the pope be not simply a name but a felt presence, sustaining the fervent plea of the Bride: *"Come, Lord!"*

Whenever a hand reaches out to do good or to show the love of Christ, to dry a tear or bring comfort to the lonely, to show the way to one who is lost or to console a broken heart, to help the fallen or to teach those thirsting for truth, to forgive or to offer a new start in God … know that the pope is at your side, the pope supports you. He puts his hand on your own, a hand wrinkled with age, but by God's grace still able to support and encourage.

My first word to you is one of thanksgiving to God for the power of the Gospel which has brought about remarkable growth of Christ's Church in these lands and enabled its generous contribution, past and present, to American society and to the world. I thank you most heartily for your generous solidarity with the Apostolic See and the support you give to the spread of the Gospel in many suffering areas of our world. I appreciate the unfailing commitment of the Church in America to the cause of life and that of the family, which is the primary reason for my present visit. I am well aware of the immense efforts you have made to welcome and integrate those immigrants who continue to look to America, like so many others before them, in the hope of enjoying its blessings of freedom and prosperity. I also appreciate the efforts which you are making to fulfill the Church's mission of education in schools at every level and in the charitable services offered by your numerous institutions. These works are often carried out without appreciation or support, often with heroic sacrifice, out of obedience to a divine mandate which we may not disobey.

I am also conscious of the courage with which you have faced difficult moments in the recent history of the Church in this country without fear of self-criticism and at the cost of mortification and great sacrifice. Nor have you been afraid to divest whatever is unessential in order to regain the authority and trust which is demanded of ministers of Christ and rightly expected by the faithful. I realize how much the pain of recent years has weighed upon you and I have supported your generous commitment to bring healing to victims — in the knowledge that in healing we too are healed — and to work to ensure that such crimes will never be repeated.

I speak to you as the Bishop of Rome, called by God in old age, and from a land which is also American, to watch over the unity of the universal Church and to encourage in charity the journey of all the particular Churches toward ever greater knowledge, faith and love of Christ. Reading over your names, looking at your faces, knowing the extent of your churchmanship and conscious of the devotion which you have always shown for the Successor of Peter, I must tell you that I do not feel a stranger in your midst. I am a native of a land which is also vast, with great open ranges, a land which, like your own, received the faith from itinerant missionaries. I too know how hard it is to sow the Gospel among people from different worlds, with hearts often hardened by the trials of a lengthy journey. Nor am I unaware of the efforts made over the years to build up the Church amid the prairies, mountains, cities and suburbs of a frequently inhospitable land, where frontiers are always provisional and easy answers do not always work. What does work is the combination of the epic struggle of the pioneers and the homey wisdom and endurance of the settlers. As one of your poets has put it, "strong and tireless" wings combined with the wisdom of one who "knows the mountains."[1]

I do not speak to you with my voice alone, but in continuity with the words of my predecessors. From the birth of this nation, when, following the American Revolution, the first diocese was erected in Baltimore, the Church of Rome has always

---

[1] "In youth my wings were strong and tireless, / But I did not know the mountains. / In age I know the mountains / But my weary wings could not follow my vision — / Genius is wisdom and youth." (Edgar Lee Masters, *Spoon River Anthology*, "Alexander Throckmorton.")

been close to you; you have never lacked its constant assistance and encouragement. In recent decades, three popes have visited you and left behind a remarkable legacy of teaching. Their words remain timely and have helped to inspire the long-term goals which you have set for the Church in this country.

It is not my intention to offer a plan or to devise a strategy. I have not come to judge you or to lecture you. I trust completely in the voice of the One who *"will teach you all things"* (John 14:26). Allow me only, in the freedom of love, to speak to you as a brother among brothers. I have no wish to tell you what to do, because we all know what it is that the Lord asks of us. Instead, I would turn once again to the demanding task — ancient yet ever new — of seeking out the paths we need to take and the spirit with which we need to work. Without claiming to be exhaustive, I would share with you some reflections which I consider helpful for our mission.

We are bishops of the Church, shepherds appointed by God to feed his flock. Our greatest joy is to be shepherds, and only shepherds, pastors with undivided hearts and selfless devotion. We need to preserve this joy and never let ourselves be robbed of it. The evil one roars like a lion, anxious to devour it, wearing us down in our resolve to be all that we are called to be, not for ourselves but in gift and service to the *Shepherd of our souls* (cf. 1 Peter 2:25).

The heart of our identity is to be sought in constant prayer, in preaching (Acts of the Apostles 6:4) and in shepherding the flock entrusted to our care (John 21:15-17; Acts 20:28-31).

Ours must not be just any kind of prayer, but familiar union with Christ, in which we daily encounter his gaze and sense that he is asking us the question: *"Who is my mother? Who are my brothers?"* (cf. Mark 3:31-34). One in which we can calmly reply: *"Lord, here is your mother, here are your brothers! I hand them over to you; they are the ones whom you entrusted to me."* Such trusting union with Christ is what nourishes the life of a pastor.

It is not about preaching complicated doctrines, but joyfully proclaiming Christ who died and rose for our sake. The "style" of our mission should make our hearers feel that the message we preach is meant *"for us."* May the word of God grant meaning and fullness to every aspect of their lives; may the sacraments nourish them with that food which they cannot procure for themselves; may the closeness of the shepherd make them long once again for the Father's embrace. Be vigilant that the flock may always encounter in the heart of their pastor that "taste of eternity" which they seek in vain in the things of this world. May they always hear from you a word of appreciation for their efforts to confirm in liberty and justice the prosperity in which this land abounds. At the same time, may you never lack the serene courage to proclaim that *we must work not for the food which perishes, but for the food which endures for eternal life* (cf. John 6:27).

Shepherds do not pasture themselves but are able to step back, away from the center, to "decrease," in order to feed God's family with Christ. Who keep constant watch, standing on the heights to look out with God's eyes on the flock which is his alone. Who ascend to the height of the cross of God's Son, the sole standpoint which opens to the shepherd the heart of his flock.

Shepherds do not lower our gaze, concerned only with our concerns, but raise it constantly toward the horizons which God opens before us and which surpass all that we ourselves can foresee or plan. Who also watch over ourselves, so as to flee the temptation of narcissism, which blinds the eyes of the shepherd, makes his voice unrecognizable and his actions fruitless. In the countless paths which lie open to our pastoral concern, remember to keep focused on the core which unifies everything: *"You did it to me"* (Matthew 25:31-45).

Certainly it is helpful for a bishop to have the farsightedness of a leader and the shrewdness of an administrator, but we fall into hopeless decline whenever we confuse the power of strength with the strength of that powerlessness with which God has redeemed us. Bishops need to be lucidly aware of the battle between light and darkness being fought in this world. Woe to us, however, if we make of the cross a banner of worldly struggles and fail to realize that the price of lasting victory is allowing ourselves to be wounded and consumed (Philippians 2:1-11).

We all know the anguish felt by the first Eleven, huddled together, assailed and overwhelmed by the fear of sheep scattered because the shepherd had been struck. But we also know that we have been given a spirit of courage and not of timidity. So we cannot let ourselves be paralyzed by fear.

I know that you face many challenges, and that the field in which you sow is unyielding and that there is always the temptation to give in to fear, to lick one's wounds, to think back on bygone times and to devise harsh responses to fierce opposition. And yet we are promoters of the culture of encounter. We are living sacraments of the embrace between God's riches and our poverty. We are witnesses of the abasement and the condescension of God who anticipates in love our every response. Dialogue is our method, not as a shrewd strategy but out of fidelity to the One who never wearies of visiting the marketplace, even at the eleventh hour, to propose his offer of love (Matthew 20:1-16).

The path ahead, then, is dialogue among yourselves, dialogue in your presbyterates, dialogue with laypersons, dialogue with families, dialogue with society. I cannot ever tire of encouraging you to dialogue fearlessly. The richer the heritage which you are called to share with *parrhesia*, the more eloquent should be the humility with which you should offer it. Do not be afraid to set out on that "exodus" which is necessary for all authentic dialogue. Otherwise, we fail to understand the thinking of others, or to realize deep down that the brother or sister we wish to reach and redeem, with the power and the closeness of love, counts more than their positions, distant as they may be from what we hold as true and certain. Harsh and divisive language does not befit the tongue of a pastor, it has no place in his heart; although it may momentarily seem to win the day, only the enduring allure of goodness and love remains truly convincing.

We need to let the Lord's words echo constantly in our hearts: *Take my yoke upon you, and learn from me, who am meek and humble of heart, and you will find refreshment for your souls* (cf. Matthew 11:28-30). Jesus' yoke is a yoke of love and thus a pledge of refreshment. At times in our work we can be burdened by a sense of loneliness, and so feel the heaviness of the yoke that we forget that we have received it from the Lord. It seems to be ours alone, and so we drag it like weary oxen working a dry field, troubled by the thought that we are laboring in vain. We can forget the profound refreshment which is indissolubly linked to the One who has made us the promise.

We need to learn from Jesus, or better to learn Jesus, meek and humble; to enter into his meekness and his humility by contemplating his way of acting; to lead our Churches and our people — not infrequently burdened by the stress of everyday life — to the ease of the Lord's yoke. And to remember that Jesus' Church is kept whole not by *consuming fire from heaven* (cf. Luke 9:54), but by the secret warmth of the Spirit, who heals what is wounded, bends what is rigid, straightens what is crooked.

The great mission which the Lord gives us is one which we carry out in communion, collegially. The world is already so torn and divided, brokenness is now everywhere. Consequently, the Church, *"the seamless garment of the Lord,"* cannot allow herself to be rent, broken, or fought over.

Our mission as bishops is first and foremost to solidify unity, a unity whose content is defined by the Word of God and the one Bread of Heaven. With these two realities each of the Churches entrusted to us remains Catholic, because open to, and in communion with, all the particular Churches and with the Church of Rome which *"presides in charity."* It is imperative, therefore, to watch over that unity, to safeguard it, to promote it and to bear witness to it as a sign and instrument which, beyond every barrier, unites nations, races, classes, and generations.

May the forthcoming Holy Year of Mercy, by drawing us into the fathomless depths of God's heart in which no division dwells, be for all of you a privileged moment for strengthening communion, perfecting unity, reconciling differences, forgiving one another and healing every rift, that your light may shine forth like *"a city set on a hill"* (Matthew 5:14).

This service to unity is particularly important for this nation, whose vast material and spiritual, cultural and political, historical and human, scientific and technological resources impose significant moral responsibilities in a world which is seeking, confusedly and laboriously, new balances of peace, prosperity and integration. It is an essential part of your mission to offer to the United States of America the humble yet powerful leaven of communion. May all mankind know that the presence in its midst of the *"sacrament of unity"* (*Lumen Gentium*, 1) is a guarantee that its fate is not decay and dispersion.

This kind of witness is a beacon whose light can reassure men and women sailing through the dark clouds of life that a sure haven awaits them, that they will not crash on the reefs or be overwhelmed by the waves. I encourage you, then, my brothers, to confront the challenging issues of our time. Ever present within each of them is life as gift and responsibility. The future freedom and dignity of our societies depends on how we face these challenges.

The innocent victim of abortion, children who die of hunger or from bombings, immigrants who drown in the search for a better tomorrow, the elderly or the sick who are considered a burden, the victims of terrorism, wars, violence and drug trafficking, the environment devastated by man's predatory relationship with nature — at stake in all of this is the gift of God, of which we are noble stewards but not masters. It is wrong, then, to look the other way or to remain silent. No less important is the Gospel of the Family, which in the World Meeting of Families in Philadelphia I will emphatically proclaim together with you and the entire Church.

These essential aspects of the Church's mission belong to the core of what we have received from the Lord. It is our duty to preserve and communicate them, even when the tenor of the times becomes resistant and even hostile to that message (*Evangelii Gaudium*, 34-39). I urge you to offer this witness, with the means and creativity born of love, and with the humility of truth. It needs to be preached and proclaimed to those without, but also to find room in people's hearts and in the conscience of society.

To this end, it is important that the Church in the United States also be a humble home, a family fire which attracts men and women through the attractive light and warmth of love. As pastors, we know well how much darkness and cold there is in this world; we know the loneliness and the neglect experienced by many people, even amid great resources of communication and material wealth. We also know their fear in the face of life, their despair and the many forms of escapism to which it gives rise.

Consequently, only a Church which can gather around the family fire remains able to attract others. And not any fire, but the one which blazed forth on Easter morn. The risen Lord continues to challenge the Church's pastors through the quiet plea of so many of our brothers and sisters: *"Have you something to eat?"* We need to recognize the Lord's voice, as the apostles did on the shore of the lake of Tiberius (John 21:4-12). It becomes even more urgent to grow in the certainty that the embers of his presence, kindled in the fire of his passion, precede us and will never die out. Whenever this certainty weakens, we end up being caretakers of ash, and not guardians and dispensers of the true light and the warmth which causes our hearts to burn within us (Luke 24:32).

Before concluding, allow me to offer two recommendations which are close to my heart. The first refers to your fatherhood as bishops. Be pastors close to people, pastors who are neighbors and servants. Let this closeness be expressed in a special way towards your priests. Support them, so that they can continue to serve Christ with an undivided heart, for this alone can bring fulfillment to ministers of Christ. I urge you, then, not to let them be content with half-measures. Find ways to encourage their spiritual growth, lest they yield to the temptation to become notaries and bureaucrats, but instead reflect the motherhood of the Church, which gives birth to and raises her sons and daughters. Be vigilant lest they tire of getting up to answer those who knock on their door by night, just when they feel entitled to rest (Luke 11:5-8). Train them to be ready to stop, care for, soothe, lift up, and assist those who *"by chance"* find themselves stripped of all they thought they had (Luke 10:29-37).

My second recommendation has to do with immigrants. I ask you to excuse me if in some way I am pleading my own case.

The Church in the United States knows like few others the hopes present in the hearts of these "pilgrims." From the beginning you have learned their languages, promoted their cause, made their contributions your own, defended their rights, helped them to prosper, and kept alive the flame of their faith. Even today, no American institution does more for immigrants than your Christian communities. Now you are facing this stream of Latin immigration which affects many of your dioceses. Not only as the Bishop of Rome, but also as a pastor from the South, I feel the need to thank and encourage you. Perhaps it will not be easy for you to look into their soul; perhaps you will be challenged by their diversity. But know that they also possess resources meant to be shared. So do not be afraid to welcome them. Offer them the warmth of the love of Christ and you will unlock the mystery of their heart. I am certain that, as so often in the past, these people will enrich America and its Church.

May God bless you and Our Lady watch over you! Thank you!

XIII

Keep Moving Forward!

Mass, Canonization of
Blessed Father Junípero Serra
Homily of Pope Francis
National Shrine of the Immaculate Conception,
Washington, D.C.
Wednesday, September 23, 2015

~

Rejoice in the Lord always! I say it again, rejoice! These are striking words, words which impact our lives. Paul tells us to rejoice; he practically orders us to rejoice. This command resonates with the desire we all have for a fulfilling life, a meaningful life, a joyful life. It is as if Paul could hear what each one of us is thinking in his or her heart and to voice what we are feeling, what we are experiencing. Something deep within us invites us to rejoice and tells us not to settle for placebos which always keep us comfortable.

At the same time, though, we all know the struggles of everyday life. So much seems to stand in the way of this invitation to rejoice. Our daily routine can often lead us to a kind of glum apathy which gradually becomes a habit, with a fatal consequence: our hearts grow numb.

We don't want apathy to guide our lives ... or do we? We don't want the force of habit to rule our life ... or do we? So we ought to ask ourselves: What can we do to keep our heart from growing numb, becoming anesthetized? How do we make the joy of the Gospel increase and take deeper root in our lives?

Jesus gives the answer. He said to his disciples then, and he says it to us now: Go forth! Proclaim! The joy of the Gospel is something to be experienced, something to be known and lived only through giving it away, through giving ourselves away.

The spirit of the world tells us to be like everyone else, to settle for what comes easy. Faced with this human way of thinking, "we must regain the conviction that we need one another, that we have a shared responsibility for others and for the world" (*Laudato Si'*, 229). It is the responsibility to proclaim the message of Jesus. For the source of our joy is "an endless desire to show mercy, the fruit of our own experience of the power of the Father's infinite mercy" (*Evangelii Gaudium*, 24). Go out to all, proclaim by anointing and anoint by proclaiming. This is what the Lord tells us today. He tells us:

A Christian finds joy in mission: Go out to people of every nation!

A Christian experiences joy in following a command: Go forth and proclaim the good news!

A Christian finds ever new joy in answering a call: Go forth and anoint!

Jesus sends his disciples out to all nations, to every people. We too were part of all those people of two thousand years ago. Jesus did not provide a short list of who is, or is not, worthy of receiving his message and his presence. Instead, he always embraced life as he saw it, in faces of pain, hunger, sickness, and sin, in faces of wounds, of thirst, of weariness, doubt, and pity. Far from expecting a pretty life, smartly-dressed and neatly groomed, he embraced life as he found it. It made no difference whether it was dirty, unkempt, broken.

Jesus said: Go out and tell the good news to everyone. Go out and in my name embrace life as it is, and not as you think it should be. Go out to the highways and byways, go out to tell the good news fearlessly, without prejudice, without superiority, without condescension, to all those who have lost the joy of living. Go out to proclaim the merciful embrace of the Father. Go out to those who are burdened by pain and failure, who feel that their lives are empty, and proclaim the folly of a loving Father who wants to anoint them with the oil of hope, the oil of salvation. Go out to proclaim the good news that error, deceitful illusions and falsehoods do not have the last word in a person's life. Go out with the ointment which soothes wounds and heals hearts.

Mission is never the fruit of a perfectly planned program or a well-organized manual. Mission is always the fruit of a life which knows what it is to be found and healed, encountered and forgiven. Mission is born of a constant experience of God's merciful anointing.

The Church, the holy People of God, treads the dust-laden paths of history, so often traversed by conflict, injustice and violence, in order to encounter her children, our brothers and sisters. The holy and faithful People of God are not afraid of losing their way; they are afraid of becoming self-enclosed, frozen into elites, clinging to their own security. They know that self-enclosure, in all the many forms it takes, is the cause of so much apathy.

So let us go out, let us go forth to offer everyone the life of Jesus Christ (*Evangelii Gaudium*, 49). The People of God can embrace everyone because we are the disciples of the One who knelt before his own to wash their feet (ibid., 24).

We are here today, we can be here today, because many people wanted to respond to that call. They believed that "life grows by being given away, and it weakens in isolation and comfort" (*Aparecida Document*, 360). We are heirs to the bold missionary spirit of so many men and women who preferred not to be "shut up within structures which give us a false sense of security … within habits which make us feel safe, while at our door people are starving" (*Evangelii Gaudium*, 49). We are indebted to a tradition, a chain of witnesses who have made it possible for the good news of the Gospel to be, in every generation, both "good" and "news."

Today we remember one of those witnesses who testified to the joy of the Gospel in these lands, Father Junípero Serra. He was the embodiment of "a Church which goes forth," a Church which sets out to bring everywhere the reconciling tenderness of God. Junípero Serra left his native land and its way of life. He was excited about blazing trails, going forth to meet many people, learning and valuing their particular customs and ways of life. He learned how to bring to birth and nurture God's life in the faces of everyone he met; he made them his brothers and sisters. Junípero sought to defend the dignity of the native community, to protect it from those who had mistreated and abused it. Mistreatment and wrongs which today still trouble us, especially because of the hurt which they cause in the lives of many people.

Father Serra had a motto which inspired his life and work, not just a saying, but above all a reality which shaped the way he lived: *siempre adelante*! Keep moving forward! For him, this was the way to continue experiencing the joy of the Gospel, to keep his heart from growing numb, from being anesthetized. He kept moving forward, because the Lord was waiting. He kept going, because his brothers and sisters were waiting. He kept going forward to the end of his life. Today, like him, may we be able to say: Forward! Let's keep moving forward!

XIV

Address to Joint Session of the United States Congress

Visit to Joint Session of the
United States Congress
Address of Pope Francis
United States Capitol, Washington, D.C.
Thursday, September 24, 2015

~

Mr. Vice-President,
Mr. Speaker,
Honorable Members of Congress,
Dear Friends,

I am most grateful for your invitation to address this Joint Session of Congress in "the land of the free and the home of the brave." I would like to think that the reason for this is that I too am a son of this great continent, from which we have all received so much and toward which we share a common responsibility.

Each son or daughter of a given country has a mission, a personal and social responsibility. Your own responsibility as members of Congress is to enable this country, by your legislative activity, to grow as a nation. You are the face of its people, their representatives. You are called to defend and preserve the dignity of your fellow citizens in the tireless and demanding pursuit of the common good, for this is the chief aim of all politics. A political society endures when it seeks, as a vocation, to satisfy common needs by stimulating the growth of all its members, especially those in situations of greater vulnerability or risk. Legislative activity is always based on care for the people. To this you have been invited, called and convened by those who elected you.

Yours is a work which makes me reflect in two ways on the figure of Moses. On the one hand, the patriarch and lawgiver of the people of Israel symbolizes the need of peoples to keep alive their sense of unity by means of just legislation. On the other, the figure of Moses leads us directly to God and thus to the transcendent dignity of the human being. Moses provides us with a good synthesis of your work: you are asked to protect, by means of the law, the image and likeness fashioned by God on every human face.

Today I would like not only to address you, but through you the entire people of the United States. Here, together with their representatives, I would like to take this opportunity to dialogue with the many thousands of men and women who strive each day to do an honest day's work, to bring home their daily bread, to save money, and — one step at a time — to build a better life for their families. These are men and women who are not concerned simply with paying their taxes, but in their own quiet way sustain the life of society. They generate solidarity by their actions, and they create organizations which offer a helping hand to those most in need.

I would also like to enter into dialogue with the many elderly persons who are a storehouse of wisdom forged by experience, and who seek in many ways, especially through volunteer work, to share their stories and their insights. I know that many of them are retired, but still active; they keep working to build up this land. I also want to dialogue with all those young people who are working to realize their great and noble aspirations, who are not led astray by facile proposals, and who face difficult situations, often as a result of immaturity on the part of many adults. I wish to dialogue with all of you, and I would like to do so through the historical memory of your people.

My visit takes place at a time when men and women of good will are marking the anniversaries of several great Americans. The complexities of history and the reality of human weakness notwithstanding, these men and women, for all their many

differences and limitations, were able by hard work and self-sacrifice — some at the cost of their lives — to build a better future.
They shaped fundamental values which will endure forever in the
spirit of the American people. A people with this spirit can live
through many crises, tensions and conflicts, while always finding
the resources to move forward, and to do so with dignity. These
men and women offer us a way of seeing and interpreting reality.
In honoring their memory, we are inspired, even amid conflicts,
and in the here and now of each day, to draw upon our deepest
cultural reserves.

I would like to mention four of these Americans: Abraham
Lincoln, Martin Luther King, Dorothy Day, and Thomas Merton.

This year marks the one hundred and fiftieth anniversary
of the assassination of President Abraham Lincoln, the guardian
of liberty, who labored tirelessly that "this nation, under God,
[might] have a new birth of freedom." Building a future of freedom requires love of the common good and cooperation in a
spirit of subsidiarity and solidarity.

All of us are quite aware of, and deeply worried by, the
disturbing social and political situation of the world today. Our
world is increasingly a place of violent conflict, hatred and brutal
atrocities, committed even in the name of God and of religion.
We know that no religion is immune from forms of individual
delusion or ideological extremism. This means that we must be
especially attentive to every type of fundamentalism, whether
religious or of any other kind. A delicate balance is required to
combat violence perpetrated in the name of a religion, an ideology or an economic system, while also safeguarding religious freedom, intellectual freedom and individual freedoms. But there is
another temptation which we must especially guard against: the
simplistic reductionism which sees only good or evil; or, if you
will, the righteous and sinners.

The contemporary world, with its open wounds which affect so many of our brothers and sisters, demands that we confront every form of polarization which would divide it into these
two camps. We know that in the attempt to be freed of the en-

emy without, we can be tempted to feed the enemy within. To imitate the hatred and violence of tyrants and murderers is the best way to take their place. That is something which you, as a people, reject.

Our response must instead be one of hope and healing, of peace and justice. We are asked to summon the courage and the intelligence to resolve today's many geopolitical and economic crises. Even in the developed world, the effects of unjust structures and actions are all too apparent. Our efforts must aim at restoring hope, righting wrongs, maintaining commitments, and thus promoting the well-being of individuals and of peoples. We must move forward together, as one, in a renewed spirit of fraternity and solidarity, cooperating generously for the common good.

The challenges facing us today call for a renewal of that spirit of cooperation, which has accomplished so much good throughout the history of the United States. The complexity, the gravity and the urgency of these challenges demand that we pool our resources and talents, and resolve to support one another, with respect for our differences and our convictions of conscience.

In this land, the various religious denominations have greatly contributed to building and strengthening society. It is important that today, as in the past, the voice of faith continue to be heard, for it is a voice of fraternity and love, which tries to bring out the best in each person and in each society. Such cooperation is a powerful resource in the battle to eliminate new global forms of slavery, born of grave injustices which can be overcome only through new policies and new forms of social consensus.

Here I think of the political history of the United States, where democracy is deeply rooted in the mind of the American people. All political activity must serve and promote the good of the human person and be based on respect for his or her dignity. "We hold these truths to be self-evident, that all men are created equal, that they are endowed by their Creator with certain unalienable Rights, that among these are Life, Liberty, and the pursuit of Happiness" (*Declaration of Independence*, July 4, 1776). If politics must truly be at the service of the human person, it follows that it cannot be a slave to the economy and finance. Politics is, instead, an expression of our compelling need to live as one, in order to build as one the greatest common good: that of a community which sacrifices particular interests in order to share, in justice and peace, its goods, its interests, its social life. I do not underestimate the difficulty that this involves, but I encourage you in this effort.

Here too I think of the march which Martin Luther King led from Selma to Montgomery fifty years ago as part of the campaign to fulfill his "dream" of full civil and political rights for African-Americans. That dream continues to inspire us all. I am happy that America continues to be, for many, a land of "dreams," dreams which lead to action, to participation, to commitment, dreams which awaken what is deepest and truest in the life of a people.

In recent centuries, millions of people came to this land to pursue their dream of building a future in freedom. We, the people of this continent, are not fearful of foreigners, because most of us were once foreigners. I say this to you as the son of immigrants, knowing that so many of you are also descended from immigrants. Tragically, the rights of those who were here long before us were not always respected. For those peoples and their nations, from the heart of American democracy, I wish to reaffirm my highest esteem and appreciation. Those first contacts were often turbulent and violent, but it is difficult to judge the past by the criteria of the present. Nonetheless, when the stranger in our midst appeals to us, we must not repeat the sins and the errors of the past. We must resolve now to live as nobly and as justly as possible, as we educate new generations not to turn their back on our "neighbors" and everything around us. Building a nation calls us to recognize that we must constantly relate to others, rejecting a mindset of hostility in order to adopt one of reciprocal subsidiarity, in a constant effort to do our best. I am confident that we can do this.

Our world is facing a refugee crisis of a magnitude not seen since the Second World War. This presents us with great challenges and many hard decisions. On this continent, too, thousands of persons are led to travel north in search of a better life for themselves and for their loved ones, in search of greater opportunities. Is this not what we want for our own children? We must not be taken aback by their numbers, but rather view them as persons, seeing their faces and listening to their stories, trying to respond as best we can to their situation, to respond in a way which is always humane, just, and fraternal. We need to avoid a common temptation nowadays: to discard whatever proves troublesome. Let us remember the Golden Rule: "Do unto others as you would have them do unto you" (cf. Matthew 7:12).

This Rule points us in a clear direction. Let us treat others with the same passion and compassion with which we want to be treated. Let us seek for others the same possibilities which we seek for ourselves. Let us help others to grow, as we would like to be helped ourselves. In a word, if we want security, let us give security; if we want life, let us give life; if we want opportunities, let us provide opportunities. The yardstick we use for others will be the yardstick which time will use for us. The Golden Rule also reminds us of our responsibility to protect and defend human life at every stage of its development.

This conviction has led me, from the beginning of my ministry, to advocate at different levels for the global abolition of the death penalty. I am convinced that this way is the best, since every life is sacred, every human person is endowed with an inalienable dignity, and society can only benefit from the rehabilitation of those convicted of crimes. Recently my brother bishops here in the United States renewed their call for the abolition of the death penalty. Not only do I support them, but I also offer encouragement to all those who are convinced that a just and necessary punishment must never exclude the dimension of hope and the goal of rehabilitation.

In these times when social concerns are so important, I cannot fail to mention the Servant of God Dorothy Day, who founded the *Catholic Worker Movement*. Her social activism, her passion for justice and for the cause of the oppressed, were inspired by the Gospel, her faith, and the example of the saints.

How much progress has been made in this area in so many parts of the world! How much has been done in these first years of the third millennium to raise people out of extreme poverty! I know that you share my conviction that much more still needs to be done, and that in times of crisis and economic hardship a spirit of global solidarity must not be lost. At the same time I would encourage you to keep in mind all those people around us who are trapped in a cycle of poverty. They too need to be given hope. The fight against poverty and hunger must be fought constantly and on many fronts, especially in its causes. I know that many Americans today, as in the past, are working to deal with this problem.

It goes without saying that part of this great effort is the creation and distribution of wealth. The right use of natural resources, the proper application of technology and the harnessing of the spirit of enterprise are essential elements of an economy which seeks to be modern, inclusive and sustainable. "Business is a noble vocation, directed to producing wealth and improving our world. It can be a fruitful source of prosperity for the areas in which it operates, especially if it sees the creation of jobs as an essential part of its service to the common good" (*Laudato Si'*, 129). This common good also includes the earth, a central theme of the encyclical which I recently wrote in order to "enter into dialogue with all people about our common home" (ibid., 3). "We need a conversation which includes everyone, since the environmental challenge we are undergoing, and its human roots, concern and affect us all" (ibid., 14).

In *Laudato Si'*, I call for a courageous and responsible effort to "redirect our steps" (ibid., 61), and to avert the most serious effects of the environmental deterioration caused by human activity. I am convinced that we can make a difference and I have no doubt that the United States — and this Congress — have an important role to play. Now is the time for courageous actions and strategies, aimed at implementing a "culture of care" (ibid., 231) and "an integrated approach to combating poverty, restoring dignity to the excluded, and at the same time protecting nature" (ibid., 139). "We have the freedom needed to limit and direct technology" (ibid., 112); "to devise intelligent ways of … developing and limiting our power" (ibid., 78); and to put technology "at the service of another type of progress, one which is healthier, more human, more social, more integral" (ibid., 112). In this regard, I am confident that America's outstanding academic and research institutions can make a vital contribution in the years ahead.

A century ago, at the beginning of the Great War, which Pope Benedict XV termed a "pointless slaughter," another notable American was born: the Cistercian monk Thomas Merton. He remains a source of spiritual inspiration and a guide for many people. In his autobiography he wrote: "I came into the world. Free by nature, in the image of God, I was nevertheless the prisoner of my own violence and my own selfishness, in the image of the world into which I was born. That world was the picture of Hell, full of men like myself, loving God, and yet hating him; born to love him, living instead in fear of hopeless self-contradictory hungers." Merton was above all a man of prayer, a thinker who challenged the certitudes of his time and opened new horizons for souls and for the Church. He was also a man of dialogue, a promoter of peace between peoples and religions.

From this perspective of dialogue, I would like to recognize the efforts made in recent months to help overcome historic differences linked to painful episodes of the past. It is my duty to build bridges and to help all men and women, in any way possible, to do the same. When countries which have been at odds resume the path of dialogue — a dialogue which may have been interrupted for the most legitimate of reasons — new opportunities open up for all. This has required, and requires, courage and daring, which is not the same as irresponsibility. A good political leader is one who, with the interests of all in mind, seizes the moment in a spirit of openness and pragmatism. A good political leader always opts to initiate processes rather than possessing spaces (cf. *Evangelii Gaudium*, 222-223).

Being at the service of dialogue and peace also means being truly determined to minimize and, in the long term, to end the many armed conflicts throughout our world. Here we have to ask ourselves: Why are deadly weapons being sold to those who plan to inflict untold suffering on individuals and society? Sadly, the answer, as we all know, is simply for money: money that is drenched in blood, often innocent blood. In the face of this shameful and culpable silence, it is our duty to confront the problem and to stop the arms trade.

Three sons and a daughter of this land, four individuals and four dreams: Lincoln, liberty; Martin Luther King, liberty in plurality and non-exclusion; Dorothy Day, social justice and the rights of persons; and Thomas Merton, the capacity for dialogue and openness to God.

Four representatives of the American people.

I will end my visit to your country in Philadelphia, where I will take part in the World Meeting of Families. It is my wish that throughout my visit the family should be a recurrent theme. How essential the family has been to the building of this country! And how worthy it remains of our support and encouragement! Yet I cannot hide my concern for the family, which is threatened, perhaps as never before, from within and without. Fundamental relationships are being called into question, as is the very basis of marriage and the family. I can only reiterate the importance and, above all, the richness and the beauty of family life.

In particular, I would like to call attention to those family members who are the most vulnerable, the young. For many of them, a future filled with countless possibilities beckons, yet so many others seem disoriented and aimless, trapped in a hopeless maze of violence, abuse and despair. Their problems are our problems. We cannot avoid them. We need to face them together, to talk about them and to seek effective solutions rather than getting bogged down in discussions. At the risk of oversimplifying, we might say that we live in a culture which pressures young people not to start a family, because they lack possibilities for the future. Yet this same culture presents others with so many options that they too are dissuaded from starting a family.

A nation can be considered great when it defends liberty as Lincoln did, when it fosters a culture which enables people to "dream" of full rights for all their brothers and sisters, as Martin

Luther King sought to do; when it strives for justice and the cause of the oppressed, as Dorothy Day did by her tireless work, the fruit of a faith which becomes dialogue and sows peace in the contemplative style of Thomas Merton.

In these remarks I have sought to present some of the richness of your cultural heritage, of the spirit of the American people. It is my desire that this spirit continue to develop and grow, so that as many young people as possible can inherit and dwell in a land which has inspired so many people to dream.

God bless America!

Greeting of the Holy Father from the Porch of the United States Capitol

Good day to all of you. I thank you for your welcome and your presence. I thank the most important people here today: the children. I want to ask God to bless them. Lord, Father of us all, bless his people, bless each of them, bless their families, grant them what they need most. I ask you to pray for me and, if there are some among you who do not believe or cannot pray, I ask you please to wish me well. Thank you. Thank you very much. And God bless America!

XV

GOD DOES NOT ABANDON US

VISIT TO THE CHARITABLE CENTER OF ST. PATRICK
PARISH AND MEETING WITH THE HOMELESS
GREETING FROM POPE FRANCIS
ST. PATRICK CHURCH, WASHINGTON, D.C.
THURSDAY, SEPTEMBER 24, 2015

~

It is a pleasure to meet you. Good day. You are about to listen to two sermons, one in Spanish and the other in English. The first word I wish to say to you is "Thank you." Thank you for welcoming me and for your efforts to make this meeting possible.

Here I think of a person whom I love very much, someone who is, and has been, very important throughout my life. He has been a support and an inspiration. He is the one I go to whenever I am "in a fix." You make me think of St. Joseph. Your faces remind me of his.

Joseph had to face some difficult situations in his life. One of them was the time when Mary was about to give birth, to have Jesus. The Bible tells us that, *while they were in Bethlehem, the time came for her to deliver her child. And she gave birth to her firstborn son and wrapped him in bands of cloth, and laid him in a manger, because there was no place for them in the inn* (cf. Luke 2:6-7).

The Bible is very clear about this: there was no room for them. I can imagine Joseph, with his wife about to have a child, with no shelter, no home, no place to stay. The Son of God came into this world as a homeless person. The Son of God knew what it was to start life without a roof over his head. We can imagine what Joseph must have been thinking. How is it that the Son of God has no home? Why are we homeless, why don't we have housing? These are questions which many of you may ask, and do ask, every day. Like St. Joseph, you may ask: Why are we homeless, without a place to live? And those of us who do have a home, a roof over our heads, would also do well to ask: Why do these, our brothers and sisters, have no place to live? Why are these brothers and sisters of ours homeless?

Joseph's questions are timely even today; they accompany all those who throughout history have been, and are, homeless. Joseph was someone who asked questions, but first and foremost, he was a man of faith. Faith gave Joseph the power to find light just at the moment when everything seemed dark. Faith sustained him amid the troubles of life. Thanks to faith, Joseph was able to press forward when everything seemed to be holding him back.

In the face of unjust and painful situations, faith brings us the light which scatters the darkness. As it did for Joseph, faith makes us open to the quiet presence of God at every moment of our lives, in every person and in every situation. God is present in every one of you, in each one of us. I want to be very clear. There is no social or moral justification, no justification whatsoever, for lack of housing. There are many unjust situations, but we know that God is suffering with us, experiencing them at our side. He does not abandon us.

Jesus not only wanted to show solidarity with every person. He not only wanted everyone to experience his companionship, his help, his love. He identified with all those who suffer, who weep, who suffer any kind of injustice. He says this clearly: "I was hungry and you gave me food, I was thirsty and you gave me drink, I was a stranger and you welcomed me" (Matthew 25:35).

Faith makes us know that God is at our side, that God is in our midst and his presence spurs us to charity. Charity is born of the call of a God who continues to knock on our door, the door of all people, to invite us to love, to compassion, to service of one another.

Jesus keeps knocking on our doors, the doors of our lives. He doesn't do this by magic, with special effects, with flashing lights and fireworks. Jesus keeps knocking on our door in the faces of our brothers and sisters, in the faces of our neighbors, in the faces of those at our side.

Dear friends, one of the most effective ways we have to help is that of prayer. Prayer unites us; it makes us brothers and sisters. It opens our hearts and reminds us of a beautiful truth which we sometimes forget. In prayer, we all learn to say "Father," "Dad." And when we say "Father," "Dad," we learn to see one another as brothers and sisters. In prayer, there are no rich or poor, there are sons and daughters, sisters and brothers. In prayer, there is no first or second class, there is brotherhood. In prayer our hearts find the strength not to be cold and insensitive in the face of situations of injustice. In prayer, God keeps calling us, opening our hearts to charity.

How good it is for us to pray together. How good it is to encounter one another in this place where we see one another as brothers and sisters, where we realize that we need one another. Today I want to pray with you, I want to join with you, because I need your support, your closeness. I would like to invite you to pray together, for one another, with one another. That way we can keep helping one another to experience with joy that Jesus is in our midst, and that Jesus helps us to find solutions to the injustices which he himself already experienced. Not having a home.

Are you ready to pray together? I will begin in Spanish and you follow in English.

Our Father, who art in heaven ...

Before leaving you, I would like to give you God's blessing:

The LORD bless you and keep you;
the LORD make his face to shine upon you, and be gracious to
you;
the LORD lift up his countenance upon you, and give you
peace. (Numbers 6:24-26)

And, please, don't forget to pray for me. Thank you.

XVI

Gratitude and Hard Work: Two Pillars of the Spiritual Life

Vespers with Priests and Religious
Homily of Pope Francis
St. Patrick's Cathedral, New York City
Thursday, September 24, 2015

I have two thoughts today for my Muslim brothers and sisters. First, my good wishes as you celebrate today the day of sacrifice. I wish my greetings could have been warmer. Second, my closeness, on account of the tragedy which your people experienced today in Mecca.[2] In this moment of prayer, I join, and all of us join, in praying to God, our almighty and merciful Father.

We have heard the Apostle say: *There is a cause for rejoicing here, although you may for a time have to suffer the distress of many trials* (cf. 1 Peter 1:6). These words remind us of something essential. Our vocation is to be lived in joy.

This beautiful Cathedral of St. Patrick, built up over many years through the sacrifices of many men and women, can serve as a symbol of the work of generations of American priests and religious and lay faithful who helped build up the Church in the United States. In the field of education alone, how many priests and religious in this country played a central role, assisting parents in handing on to their children the food that nourishes them for life! Many did so at the cost of extraordinary sacrifice and with heroic charity. I think for example of St. Elizabeth Ann Seton, who founded the first free Catholic school for girls in

---

[2] Over 700 pilgrims from around the world were trampled to death during the annual Islamic pilgrimage to Mecca in Saudi Arabia.

America, or St. John Neumann, the founder of the first system of Catholic education in the United States.

This evening, my brothers and sisters, I have come to join you — priests and men and women of consecrated life — in praying that our vocations will continue to build up the great edifice of God's kingdom in this country. I know that, as a presbyterate in the midst of God's people, you suffered greatly in the not distant past by having to bear the shame of some of your brothers who harmed and scandalized the Church in the most vulnerable of her members.... In the words of the Book of Revelation, I say that you "have come out of the great tribulation" (Revelation 7:14). I accompany you at this moment of pain and difficulty, and I thank God for your faithful service to his people. In the hope of helping you to persevere on the path of fidelity to Jesus Christ, I would like to offer two brief reflections.

The first concerns *the spirit of gratitude*. The joy of men and women who love God attracts others to him; priests and religious are called to find and radiate lasting satisfaction in their vocation. Joy springs from a grateful heart. Truly, we have received much, so many graces, so many blessings, and we rejoice in this. It will do us good to think back on our lives with the grace of remembrance. Remembrance of when we were first called, remembrance of the road travelled, remembrance of graces received ... and, above all, remembrance of our encounter with Jesus Christ so often along the way. Remembrance of the amazement which our encounter with Jesus Christ awakens in our hearts. My brothers and sisters, men and women of consecrated life, and priests! Let us seek the grace of remembrance so as to grow in the spirit of gratitude. Let us ask ourselves: are we good at counting our blessings, or have we forgotten them?

A second area is *the spirit of hard work*. A grateful heart is spontaneously impelled to serve the Lord and to find expression in a life of commitment to our work. Once we come to realize how much God has given us, a life of self-sacrifice, of working for him and for others, becomes a privileged way of responding to his great love.

Yet, if we are honest, we know how easily this spirit of generous self-sacrifice can be dampened. There are a couple of ways that this can happen; both ways are examples of that "spiritual worldliness" which weakens our commitment as men and women of consecrated life to serve, and diminishes the wonder, the amazement, of our first encounter with Christ.

We can get caught up measuring the value of our apostolic works by the standards of efficiency, good management, and outward success which govern the business world. Not that these things are unimportant! We have been entrusted with a great responsibility, and God's people rightly expect accountability from us. But the true worth of our apostolate is measured by the value it has in God's eyes. To see and evaluate things from God's perspective calls for constant conversion in the first days and years of our vocation and, need I say, it calls for great humility. The cross shows us a different way of measuring success. Ours is to plant the seeds: God sees to the fruits of our labors. And if at times our efforts and works seem to fail and produce no fruit, we need to remember that we are followers of Jesus ... and his life, humanly speaking, ended in failure, in the failure of the cross.

The other danger comes when we become jealous of our free time, when we think that surrounding ourselves with worldly comforts will help us serve better. The problem with this reasoning is that it can blunt the power of God's daily call to conversion, to encounter with him. Slowly but surely, it diminishes our spirit of sacrifice, our spirit of renunciation and hard work. It also alienates people who suffer material poverty and are forced to make greater sacrifices than ourselves, without being consecrated. Rest is needed, as are moments of leisure and self-enrichment, but we need to learn how to rest in a way that deepens our desire to serve with generosity. Closeness to the poor, the refugee, the immigrant, the sick, the exploited, the elderly living alone, prisoners and all God's other poor, will teach us a different way of resting, one which is more Christian and generous.

Gratitude and hard work: these are two pillars of the spiritual life which I have wanted, this evening, to share with you priests and religious. I thank you for prayers and work, and the daily sacrifices you make in the various areas of your apostolate. Many of these are known only to God, but they bear rich fruit for the life of the Church.

In a special way I would like to express my esteem and my gratitude to the religious women of the United States. What would the Church be without you? Women of strength, fighters, with that spirit of courage which puts you in the front lines in the proclamation of the Gospel. To you, religious women, sisters and mothers of this people, I wish to say "thank you," a big thank you … and to tell you that I love you very much.

I know that many of you are in the front lines in meeting the challenges of adapting to an evolving pastoral landscape. Whatever difficulties and trials you face, I ask you, like St. Peter, to be at peace and to respond to them as Christ did: he thanked the Father, took up his cross, and looked forward!

Dear brothers and sisters, shortly, in a few minutes, we will sing the *Magnificat*. Let us commend to Our Lady the work we have been entrusted to do; let us join her in thanking God for the great things he has done, and for the great things he will continue to do in us and in those whom we have the privilege to serve. Amen.

XVII

WORK *FOR* PEACE, *IN* PEACE

MEETING WITH THE PERSONNEL OF THE
UNITED NATIONS
GREETING FROM POPE FRANCIS
UNITED NATIONS HEADQUARTERS, NEW YORK CITY
FRIDAY, SEPTEMBER 25, 2015

~

Dear Friends,

On the occasion of my visit to the United Nations, I am pleased to greet you, the men and women who are, in many ways, the backbone of this organization. I thank you for your welcome, and I am grateful for all that you have done to prepare for my visit. I would ask you also to offer my greetings to the members of your families and to your colleagues who could not be with us today.

The vast majority of the work done here is not of the kind that makes the news. Behind the scenes, your daily efforts make possible many of the diplomatic, cultural, economic, and political initiatives of the United Nations, which are so important for meeting the hopes and expectations of the peoples who make up our human family. You are experts and experienced fieldworkers, officials and secretaries, translators and interpreters, cleaners and cooks, maintenance and security personnel. Thank you for all that you do! Your quiet and devoted work not only contributes to the betterment of the United Nations, it also has great significance for you personally. For how we work expresses our dignity and the kind of persons we are.

Many of you have come to this city from countries the world over. As such, you are a microcosm of the peoples which this organization represents and seeks to serve. Like so many other people worldwide, you are concerned about your children's welfare and education. You worry about the future of the planet, and what kind of a world we will leave for future generations. But today, and every day, I would ask each of you, whatever your capacity, to care for one another. Be close to one another, respect one another, and so embody among yourselves this organization's ideal of a united human family, living in harmony, working not only *for* peace, but *in* peace; working not only *for* justice, but in a *spirit* of justice.

Dear friends, I bless each one of you from my heart. I will pray for you and your families, and I ask each of you, please, to remember to pray for me. And if any of you are not believers, I ask you to wish me well. God bless you all.

Thank you.

XVIII

ADDRESS TO THE UNITED NATIONS GENERAL ASSEMBLY

MEETING WITH THE MEMBERS OF THE GENERAL
ASSEMBLY OF THE UNITED NATIONS
ADDRESS OF POPE FRANCIS
UNITED NATIONS HEADQUARTERS, NEW YORK CITY
FRIDAY, SEPTEMBER 25, 2015

~

Mr. President,
Ladies and Gentlemen,

Good day. Once again, following a tradition by which I feel honored, the Secretary General of the United Nations has invited the pope to address this distinguished assembly of nations. In my own name, and that of the entire Catholic community, I wish to express to you, Mr. Ban Ki-moon, my heartfelt gratitude. I greet the Heads of State and Heads of Government present, as well as the ambassadors, diplomats, and political and technical officials accompanying them, the personnel of the United Nations engaged in this seventieth Session of the General Assembly, the personnel of the various programs and agencies of the United Nations family, and all those who, in one way or another, take part in this meeting. Through you, I also greet the citizens of all the nations represented in this hall. I thank you, each and all, for your efforts in the service of mankind.

This is the fifth time that a pope has visited the United Nations. I follow in the footsteps of my predecessors Paul VI, in 1965, John Paul II, in 1979 and 1995, and my most recent predecessor, now Pope Emeritus Benedict XVI, in 2008. All of them expressed their great esteem for the organization, which they considered the appropriate juridical and political response to this present moment of history, marked by our technical ability to overcome distances and frontiers and, apparently, to overcome all natural limits to the exercise of power. An essential response, inasmuch as technological power, in the hands of nationalistic or falsely universalist ideologies, is capable of perpetrating tremendous atrocities. I can only reiterate the appreciation expressed by my predecessors, in reaffirming the importance which the Catholic Church attaches to this institution and the hope which she places in its activities.

The United Nations is presently celebrating its seventieth anniversary. The history of this organized community of states is one of important common achievements over a period of unusually fast-paced changes. Without claiming to be exhaustive, we can mention the codification and development of international law, the establishment of international norms regarding human rights, advances in humanitarian law, the resolution of numerous conflicts, operations of peacekeeping and reconciliation, and any number of other accomplishments in every area of international activity and endeavor. All these achievements are lights which help to dispel the darkness of the disorder caused by unrestrained ambitions and collective forms of selfishness. Certainly, many grave problems remain to be resolved, yet it is also clear that, without all this international activity, mankind would not have been able to survive the unchecked use of its own possibilities. Every one of these political, juridical, and technical advances is a path towards attaining the ideal of human fraternity and a means for its greater realization.

I also pay homage to all those men and women whose loyalty and self-sacrifice have benefitted humanity as a whole in these past seventy years. In particular, I would recall today those who gave their lives for peace and reconciliation among peoples, from Dag Hammarskjöld to the many United Nations officials at every level who have been killed in the course of humanitarian missions and missions of peace and reconciliation.

Beyond these achievements, the experience of the past seventy years has made it clear that reform and adaptation to the times is always necessary in the pursuit of the ultimate goal of granting all countries, without exception, a share in, and a genuine and equitable influence on, decision-making processes. The need for greater equity is especially true in the case of those bodies with effective executive capability, such as the Security Council, the Financial Agencies, and the groups or mechanisms specifically created to deal with economic crises. This will help limit every kind of abuse or usury, especially where developing countries are concerned. The International Financial Agencies should care for the sustainable development of countries and should ensure that they are not subjected to oppressive lending systems which, far from promoting progress, subject people to mechanisms which generate greater poverty, exclusion, and dependence.

The work of the United Nations, according to the principles set forth in the Preamble and the first Articles of its founding Charter, can be seen as the development and promotion of the rule of law, based on the realization that justice is an essential condition for achieving the ideal of universal fraternity. In this context, it is helpful to recall that the limitation of power is an idea implicit in the concept of law itself. To give to each his own, to cite the classic definition of justice, means that no human individual or group can consider itself absolute, permitted to bypass the dignity and the rights of other individuals or their social groupings.

The effective distribution of power (political, economic, defense-related, technological, etc.) among a plurality of subjects and the creation of a juridical system for regulating claims and interests [is] one concrete way of limiting power. Yet today's world presents us with many false rights and — at the same time — broad sectors which are vulnerable, victims of power badly exercised: for example, the natural environment and the vast ranks of the excluded. These sectors are closely interconnected and made increasingly fragile by dominant political and economic relationships. That is why their rights must be forcefully affirmed by working to protect the environment and by putting an end to exclusion.

First, it must be stated that a true "right of the environment" does exist, for two reasons; first, because we human beings are part of the environment. We live in communion with it, since the environment itself entails ethical limits which human activity must acknowledge and respect. Man, for all his remarkable gifts, which "are signs of a uniqueness which transcends the spheres of physics and biology" (*Laudato Si'*, 81), is at the same time a part of these spheres. He possesses a body shaped by physical, chemical, and biological elements and can only survive and develop if the ecological environment is favorable. Any harm done to the environment, therefore, is harm done to humanity. Second, because every creature, particularly a living creature, has an intrinsic value in its existence, its life, its beauty, and its interdependence with other creatures. We Christians, together with the other monotheistic religions, believe that the universe is the fruit of a loving decision by the Creator, who permits man respectfully to use creation for the good of his fellow men and for the glory of the Creator; he is not authorized to abuse it, much less to destroy it. In all religions, the environment is a fundamental good (cf. ibid.).

The misuse and destruction of the environment are also accompanied by a relentless process of exclusion. In effect, a selfish and boundless thirst for power and material prosperity leads both to the misuse of available natural resources and to the exclusion of the weak and disadvantaged, either because they are differently abled (handicapped), or because they lack adequate information and technical expertise or are incapable of decisive political action. Economic and social exclusion is a complete denial of human fraternity and a grave offense against human rights and the environment. The poorest are those who suffer most from such offenses, for three serious reasons: they are cast off by society, forced to live off what is discarded, and suffer unjustly from the abuse of the environment. They are part of today's widespread and quietly growing "culture of waste."

The dramatic reality this whole situation of exclusion and inequality, with its evident effects, has led me, in union with the entire Christian people and many others, to take stock of my grave responsibility in this regard and to speak out, together with all those who are seeking urgently-needed and effective solutions. The adoption of the 2030 Agenda for Sustainable Development at the World Summit, which opens today, is an important sign of hope. I am similarly confident that the Paris Conference on Climatic Change will secure fundamental and effective agreements.

Solemn commitments, however, are not enough, although they are certainly a necessary step toward solutions. The classic definition of justice which I mentioned earlier contains as one of its essential elements a constant and perpetual will: *Iustitia est constans et perpetua voluntas ius suum cuique tribuendi.* Our world demands of all government leaders a will which is effective, practical, and constant, concrete steps and immediate measures for preserving and improving the natural environment and thus putting an end as quickly as possible to the phenomenon of social and economic exclusion, with its baneful consequences: human trafficking, the marketing of human organs and tissues, the sexual exploitation of boys and girls, slave labor, including prostitution, the drug and weapons trade, terrorism, and international organized crime. Such is the magnitude of these situations and their toll in innocent lives that we must avoid every temptation to fall into a declarationist nominalism which would assuage our consciences. We need to ensure that our institutions are truly effective in the struggle against all these scourges.

The number and complexity of the problems require that we possess technical instruments of verification. But this involves two risks. We can rest content with the bureaucratic exercise of drawing up long lists of good proposals — goals, objectives, and statistics — or we can think that a single theoretical and aprioristic solution will provide an answer to all the challenges. It must never be forgotten that political and economic activity is only effective when it is understood as a prudential activity, guided by a perennial concept of justice and constantly conscious of the fact that, above and beyond our plans and programs, we are dealing with real men and women who live, struggle, and suffer and are often forced to live in great poverty, deprived of all rights.

To enable these real men and women to escape from extreme poverty, we must allow them to be dignified agents of their own destiny. Integral human development and the full exercise of human dignity cannot be imposed. They must be built up and allowed to unfold for each individual, for every family, in communion with others, and in a right relationship with all those areas in which human social life develops — friends, communities, towns and cities, schools, businesses and unions, provinces, nations, etc. This presupposes and requires the right to education — also for girls (excluded in certain places) — which is ensured first and foremost by respecting and reinforcing the primary right of the family to educate its children, as well as the right of churches and social groups to support and assist families in the education of their children. Education conceived in this way is the basis for the implementation of the 2030 Agenda and for reclaiming the environment.

At the same time, government leaders must do everything possible to ensure that all can have the minimum spiritual and material means needed to live in dignity and to create and support a family, which is the primary cell of any social development. In practical terms, this absolute minimum has three names: lodging, labor, and land; and one spiritual name: spiritual freedom, which includes religious freedom, the right to education, and all other civil rights.

For all this, the simplest and best measure and indicator of the implementation of the new *Agenda* for development will be effective, practical, and immediate access, on the part of all, to essential material and spiritual goods: housing, dignified and properly remunerated employment, adequate food and drinking water, religious freedom and, more generally, spiritual freedom, and education. These pillars of integral human development have a common foundation, which is the right to life and, more generally, what we could call the right to existence of human nature itself.

The ecological crisis and the large-scale destruction of biodiversity can threaten the very existence of the human species. The baneful consequences of an irresponsible mismanagement of the global economy, guided only by ambition for wealth and power, must serve as a summons to a forthright reflection on man: "man is not only a freedom which he creates for himself. Man does not create himself. He is spirit and will, but also nature" (Benedict XVI, *Address to the Bundestag*, September 22, 2011, cited in *Laudato Si'*, 6). Creation is compromised "where we ourselves have the final word.... The misuse of creation begins when we no longer recognize any instance above ourselves, when we see nothing else but ourselves" (*Address to the Clergy of the Diocese of Bolzano-Bressanone*, August 6, 2008, cited ibid.). Consequently, the defense of the environment and the fight against exclusion demand that we recognize a moral law written into human nature itself, one which includes the natural difference between man and woman (cf. *Laudato Si'*, 155) and absolute respect for life in all its stages and dimensions (cf. ibid., 123, 136).

Without the recognition of certain incontestable natural ethical limits and without the immediate implementation of those pillars of integral human development, the ideal of "saving succeeding generations from the scourge of war" (*Charter of the United Nations*, Preamble). and "promoting social progress and better standards of life in larger freedom" (ibid.), risks becoming an unattainable illusion, or, even worse, idle chatter which serves as a cover for all kinds of abuse and corruption, or for carrying out an ideological colonization by the imposition of anomalous models and lifestyles which are alien to people's identity and, in the end, irresponsible.

War is the negation of all rights and a dramatic assault on the environment. If we want true integral human development for all, we must work tirelessly to avoid war between nations and peoples.

To this end, there is a need to ensure the uncontested rule of law and tireless recourse to negotiation, mediation, and arbitration, as proposed by the *Charter of the United Nations*, which constitutes truly a fundamental juridical norm. The experience of these seventy years since the founding of the United Nations in general, and in particular the experience of these first fifteen years of the third millennium, reveal both the effectiveness of the full application of international norms and the ineffectiveness of their lack of enforcement. When the *Charter of the United Nations* is respected and applied with transparency and sincerity, and without ulterior motives, as an obligatory reference point of justice and not as a means of masking spurious intentions, peaceful results will be obtained. When, on the other hand, the norm is considered simply as an instrument to be used whenever it proves favorable, and to be avoided when it is not, a true Pandora's box is opened, releasing uncontrollable forces which gravely harm defenseless populations, the cultural milieu, and even the biological environment.

The Preamble and the first Article of the *Charter of the United Nations* set forth the foundations of the international juridical framework: peace, the pacific solution of disputes, and the development of friendly relations between the nations. Strongly opposed to such statements, and in practice denying them, is the constant tendency to the proliferation of arms, especially weapons of mass distraction such as nuclear weapons. An ethic and a law based on the threat of mutual destruction — and possibly the destruction of all mankind — are self-contradictory and an affront to the entire framework of the United Nations, which would end up as "nations united by fear and distrust." There is urgent need to work for a world free of nuclear weapons, in full application of the non-proliferation treaty, in letter and spirit, with the goal of a complete prohibition of these weapons.

The recent agreement reached on the nuclear question in a sensitive region of Asia and the Middle East is proof of the potential of political good will and of law, exercised with sincerity, patience, and constancy. I express my hope that this agreement will be lasting and efficacious and bring forth the desired fruits with the cooperation of all the parties involved.

In this sense, hard evidence is not lacking of the negative effects of military and political interventions which are not coordinated between members of the international community.

For this reason, while regretting to have to do so, I must renew my repeated appeals regarding the painful situation of the entire Middle East, North Africa, and other African countries, where Christians, together with other cultural or ethnic groups, and even members of the majority religion who have no desire to be caught up in hatred and folly, have been forced to witness the destruction of their places of worship, their cultural and religious heritage, their houses and property, and have faced the alternative either of fleeing or of paying for their adhesion to good and to peace by their own lives or by enslavement.

These realities should serve as a grave summons to an examination of conscience on the part of those charged with the conduct of international affairs. Not only in cases of religious or cultural persecution, but in every situation of conflict, as in Ukraine, Syria, Iraq, Libya, South Sudan, and the Great Lakes region, real human beings take precedence over partisan interests, however legitimate the latter may be. In wars and conflicts there are individual persons, our brothers and sisters, men and women, young and old, boys and girls who weep, suffer, and die, human beings who are easily discarded when our response is simply to draw up lists of problems, strategies, and disagreements.

As I wrote in my letter to the secretary-general of the United Nations on August 9, 2014, "The most basic understanding of human dignity compels the international community, particularly through the norms and mechanisms of international law, to do all that it can to stop and to prevent further systematic violence against ethnic and religious minorities" and to protect innocent peoples.

Along the same lines I would mention another kind of conflict, which is not always so open, yet is silently killing millions of people. Another kind of war experienced by many of our societies as a result of the narcotics trade. A war which is taken for granted and poorly fought. Drug trafficking is by its very nature accompanied by trafficking in persons, money laundering, the arms trade, child exploitation, and other forms of corruption. A corruption which has penetrated to different levels of social, political, military, artistic, and religious life, and, in many cases, has given rise to a parallel structure which threatens the credibility of our institutions.

I began this speech recalling the visits of my predecessors. I would hope that my words will be taken above all as a continuation of the final words of the address of Pope Paul VI; although spoken almost exactly fifty years ago, they remain ever timely. I quote: "The hour has come when a pause, a moment of recollection, reflection, even of prayer, is absolutely needed so that we may think back over our common origin, our history, our common destiny. The appeal to the moral conscience of man has never been as necessary as it is today.... For the danger comes neither from progress nor from science; if these are used well, they can help to solve a great number of the serious problems besetting mankind" (*Address to the United Nations Organization*, October 4, 1965). Among other things, human genius, well applied, will surely help to meet the grave challenges of ecological deterioration and of exclusion. As Paul VI said: "The real danger comes from man, who has at his disposal ever more powerful instruments that are as well fitted to bring about ruin as they are to achieve lofty conquests" (ibid.).

The common home of all men and women must continue to rise on the foundations of a right understanding of universal fraternity and respect for the sacredness of every human life, of every man and every woman, the poor, the elderly, children, the infirm, the unborn, the unemployed, the abandoned, those considered disposable because they are only considered as part of a statistic. This common home of all men and women must also be built on the understanding of a certain sacredness of created nature.

Such understanding and respect call for a higher degree of wisdom, one which accepts transcendence, self-transcendence, rejects the creation of an all-powerful elite, and recognizes that the full meaning of individual and collective life is found in selfless service to others and in the sage and respectful use of creation for the common good. To repeat the words of Paul VI, "The edifice of modern civilization has to be built on spiritual principles, for they are the only ones capable not only of supporting it, but of shedding light on it" (ibid.).

El Gaucho Martín Fierro, a classic of literature in my native land, says: "Brothers should stand by each other, because this is the first law; keep a true bond between you always, at every time — because if you fight among yourselves, you'll be devoured by those outside."

The contemporary world, so apparently connected, is experiencing a growing and steady social fragmentation, which places at risk "the foundations of social life" and consequently leads to "battles over conflicting interests" (*Laudato Si'*, 229).

The present time invites us to give priority to actions which generate new processes in society, so as to bear fruit in significant and positive historical events (cf. *Evangelii Gaudium*, 223). We cannot permit ourselves to postpone "certain agendas" for the future. The future demands of us critical and global decisions in the face of world-wide conflicts which increase the number of the excluded and those in need.

The praiseworthy international juridical framework of the United Nations Organization and of all its activities, like any other human endeavor, can be improved, yet it remains necessary; at the same time it can be the pledge of a secure and happy future for future generations. And so it will, if the representatives of the states can set aside partisan and ideological interests and sincerely strive to serve the common good. I pray to almighty God that this will be the case, and I assure you of my support and my prayers, and the support and prayers of all the faithful of the Catholic Church, that this institution, all its member states, and each of its officials, will always render an effective service to mankind, a service respectful of diversity and capable of bringing out, for sake of the common good, the best in each people and in every individual. God bless you all. Thank you.

XIX

Palpable Grief, Powerful Solidarity

Interreligious Meeting
Address of Pope Francis
Ground Zero Memorial, New York City
Friday, September 25, 2015

I feel many different emotions standing here at Ground Zero, where thousands of lives were taken in a senseless act of destruction. Here grief is palpable. The water we see flowing towards that empty pit reminds us of all those lives which fell prey to those who think that destruction, tearing down, is the only way to settle conflicts. It is the silent cry of those who were victims of a mindset which knows only violence, hatred, and revenge, a mindset which can only cause pain, suffering, destruction, and tears.

The flowing water is also a symbol of our tears. Tears at so much devastation and ruin, past and present. This is a place where we shed tears, we weep out of a sense of helplessness in the face of injustice, murder, and the failure to settle conflicts through dialogue. Here we mourn the wrongful and senseless loss of innocent lives because of the inability to find solutions which respect the common good. This flowing water reminds us of yesterday's tears, but also of all the tears still being shed today.

A few moments ago I met some of the families of the fallen first responders. Meeting them made me see once again how acts of destruction are never impersonal, abstract, or merely material. They always have a face, a concrete story, names. In those family members, we see the face of pain, a pain which still touches us and cries out to heaven.

At the same time, those family members showed me the other face of this attack, the other face of their grief: the power of love and remembrance, a remembrance that does not leave us empty and withdrawn. The names of so many loved ones are written around the towers' footprints. We can see them, we can touch them, and we can never forget them.

Here, amid pain and grief, we also have a palpable sense of the heroic goodness which people are capable of, those hidden reserves of strength from which we can draw. In the depths of pain and suffering, you also witnessed the heights of generosity and service. Hands reached out, lives were given. In a metropolis which might seem impersonal, faceless, lonely, you demonstrated the powerful solidarity born of mutual support, love, and self-sacrifice. No one thought about race, nationality, neighborhoods, religion, or politics. It was all about solidarity, meeting immediate needs, brotherhood. It was about being brothers and sisters. New York City firemen walked into the crumbling towers, with no concern for their own wellbeing. Many succumbed; their sacrifice enabled great numbers to be saved.

This place of death became a place of life, too, a place of saved lives, a hymn to the triumph of life over the prophets of destruction and death, to goodness over evil, to reconciliation and unity over hatred and division.

In this place of sorrow and remembrance, I am filled with hope, as I have the opportunity to join with leaders representing the many religious traditions which enrich the life of this great city. I trust that our presence together will be a powerful sign of our shared desire to be a force for reconciliation, peace, and justice in this community and throughout the world. For all our differences and disagreements, we can experience a world of peace. In opposing every attempt to create a rigid uniformity, we can and must build unity on the basis of our diversity of languages, cultures, and religions, and lift our voices against everything which would stand in the way of such unity. Together we are called to say "no" to every attempt to impose uniformity and "yes" to adversity accepted and reconciled.

This can only happen if we uproot from our hearts all feelings of hatred, vengeance, and resentment. We know that that is only possible as a gift from heaven. Here, in this place of remembrance, I would ask everyone together, each in his or her own way, to spend a moment in silence and prayer. Let us implore from on high the gift of commitment to the cause of peace. Peace in our homes, our families, our schools, and our communities. Peace in all those places where war never seems to end. Peace for those faces which have known nothing but pain. Peace throughout this world which God has given us as the home of all and a home for all. Simply PEACE. Let us pray in silence.

(A moment of silence.)

In this way, the lives of our dear ones will not be lives which will one day be forgotten. Instead, they will be present whenever we strive to be prophets not of tearing down but of building up, prophets of reconciliation, prophets of peace.

XX

PRAYER OF REMEMBRANCE

INTERRELIGIOUS MEETING
PRAYER OF REMEMBRANCE OF POPE FRANCIS
GROUND ZERO MEMORIAL, NEW YORK CITY
FRIDAY, SEPTEMBER 25, 2015

O God of love, compassion, and healing,
look on us, people of many different faiths
and religious traditions,
who gather today on this hallowed ground,
the scene of unspeakable violence and pain.

We ask you in your goodness
to give eternal light and peace
to all who died here:
the heroic first-responders,
our fire fighters, police officers,
emergency service workers,
and Port Authority personnel,
along with all the innocent men and women
who were victims of this tragedy
simply because their work or service
brought them here on September 11.

We ask you, in your compassion,
to bring healing to those who,
because of their presence here fourteen years ago,
continue to suffer from injuries and illness.

Heal, too, the pain of still-grieving families
and all who lost loved ones in this tragedy.
Give them strength to continue their lives
with courage and hope.

We are mindful as well
of those who suffered death, injury, and loss
on the same day at the Pentagon
and in Shanksville, Pennsylvania.
Our hearts are one with theirs
as our prayer embraces their pain and suffering.

God of peace, bring your peace to our violent world:
peace in the hearts of all men and women
and peace among the nations of the earth.
Turn to your way of love
those whose hearts and minds
are consumed with hatred
and who justify killing in the name of religion.

God of understanding,
overwhelmed by the magnitude of this tragedy,
we seek your light and guidance
as we confront such terrible events.

Grant that those whose lives were spared
may live so that the lives lost here
may not have been lost in vain.

Comfort and console us, strengthen us in hope,
and give us the wisdom and courage
to work tirelessly for a world
where true peace and love reign
among nations and in the hearts of all.

XXI

Where There Are Dreams, There Is Joy

Meeting with Children and Immigrant Families
Address of Pope Francis
Our Lady, Queen of Angels School
Harlem, New York City
Friday, September 25, 2015

Dear Brothers and Sisters,

Good afternoon!

I am very happy to be with you today, together with this big family which surrounds you. I see your teachers, your parents, and your family members. Thank you for letting me come, and I ask pardon from your teachers for "stealing" a few minutes of their class time. I know that you don't mind that!

They tell me that one of the nice things about this school, about your work, is that some students come from other places, and many from other countries. That is nice! Even though I know that it is not easy to have to move and find a new home, to meet new neighbors and new friends. It is not easy, but you have to start. At the beginning it can be pretty hard. Often you have to learn a new language, adjust to a new culture, even a new climate. There is so much to learn! And not just homework, but so other many things too.

The good thing is that we also make new friends. This is very important, the new friends we make. We meet people who open doors for us, who are kind to us. They offer us friendship and understanding, and they try to help us not to feel like strangers, foreigners. People work hard to help us feel at home. Even if we sometimes think back on where we came from, we meet good people who help us feel at home. How nice it is to feel that our school or the places where we gather are a second home. This is not only important for you, but also for your families. School then ends up being one big family. A family where, together with our mothers and fathers, our grandparents, our teachers and friends, we learn to help one another, to share our good qualities, to give the best of ourselves, to work as a team, for that is very important, and to pursue our dreams.

Very near here is a very important street named after a man who did a lot for other people. I want to talk a little bit about him. He was the Reverend Martin Luther King. One day he said, "I have a dream." His dream was that many children, many people, could have equal opportunities. His dream was that many children like you could get an education. He dreamed that many men and women, like yourselves, could lift their heads high, in dignity and self-sufficiency. It is beautiful to have dreams and to be able to fight for our dreams. Don't ever forget this.

Today we want to keep dreaming. We celebrate all the opportunities which enable you, and us adults too, not to lose the hope of a better world with greater possibilities. So many of the people I have met are also dreaming with you, they are dreaming of this. That is why they are doing this work. They are involved in your lives to help you move ahead. All of us dream. Always. I know that one of the dreams of your parents and teachers, and all those who help them — and Cardinal [Timothy] Dolan too, who is a good fellow — is that you can grow up and be happy. Here I see you smiling. Keep smiling and help bring joy to everyone you meet. It isn't always easy. Every home has its problems, difficult situations, sickness, but never stop dreaming so you can be happy.

All of you here, children and adults, have a right to dream, and I am very happy that here in school, in your friends and your teachers, in all who are here to help, you can find the support you need. Wherever there are dreams, wherever there is joy, Jesus is always present. Always. But who is it that sows sadness, that sows mistrust, envy, evil desires? What is his name? The devil. The devil always sows sadness, because he doesn't want us to be happy; he doesn't want us to dream. Wherever there is joy, Jesus is always present, because Jesus is joy, and he wants to help us to feel that joy every day of our lives.

Before going, I would like to give you some homework. Can I? It is just a little request, but a very important one. Please don't forget to pray for me, so that I can share with many people the joy of Jesus. And let us also pray that many other people can share joy like your own, whenever you feel supported, helped, and counseled, even when there are problems. Even then, we still feel peace in our hearts, because Jesus never abandons us.

May God bless every one of you today, and may Our Lady watch over all of you. Thank you.

Impromptu Remarks:

Don't you know any songs? Don't you know how to sing? Let's see, who is the bravest one here ... (*song*). Thank you very much. Now, all together ... one song, and then we can all pray the Our Father (*song, followed by the Our Father*). May almighty God bless you, the Father, the Son, and the Holy Spirit. (*Amen.*) Pray for me! Don't forget the homework!

XXII

GOD IS IN THE CITY

MASS, HOMILY OF POPE FRANCIS
MADISON SQUARE GARDEN, NEW YORK CITY
FRIDAY, SEPTEMBER 25, 2015

We are in Madison Square Garden, a place synonymous with this city. This is the site of important athletic, artistic and musical events attracting people not only from this city, but from the whole world. In this place, which represents both the variety and the common interests of so many different people, we have listened to the words: "The people who walked in darkness have seen a great light" (Isaiah 9:2). The people who walked — caught up in their activities and routines, amid their successes and failures, their worries and expectations — have seen a great light. The people who walked — with all their joys and hopes, their disappointments and regrets — have seen a great light. In every age, the People of God are called to contemplate this light. A light for the nations, as the elderly Simeon joyfully expressed it. A light meant to shine on every corner of this city, on our fellow citizens, on every part of our lives.

"The people who walked in darkness have seen a great light." One special quality of God's people is their ability to see, to contemplate, even in "moments of darkness," the light which Christ brings. God's faithful people can see, discern, and contemplate his living presence in the midst of life, in the midst of the city. Together with the prophet Isaiah, we can say: The people who walk, breathe, and live in the midst of smog have seen a great light, have experienced a breath of fresh air.

Living in a big city is not always easy. A multicultural context presents many complex challenges. Yet big cities are a reminder of the hidden riches present in our world: in the diversity of its cultures, traditions, and historical experiences, in the variety of its languages, costumes and cuisine. Big cities bring together all the different ways which we human beings have discovered to express the meaning of life, wherever we may be.

But big cities also conceal the faces of all those people who don't appear to belong, or are second-class citizens. In big cities, beneath the roar of traffic, beneath "the rapid pace of change," so many faces pass by unnoticed because they have no "right" to be there, no right to be part of the city. They are the foreigners, the children who go without schooling, those deprived of medical insurance, the homeless, the forgotten elderly. These people stand at the edges of our great avenues, in our streets, in deafening anonymity. They become part of an urban landscape which is more and more taken for granted, in our eyes, and especially in our hearts.

Knowing that Jesus still walks our streets, that he is part of the lives of his people, that he is involved with us in one vast history of salvation, fills us with hope. A hope which liberates us from the forces pushing us to isolation and lack of concern for the lives of others, for the life of our city. A hope which frees us from empty "connections," from abstract analyses, or sensationalist routines. A hope which is unafraid of involvement, which acts as a leaven wherever we happen to live and work. A hope which makes us see, even in the midst of smog, the presence of God as he continues to walk the streets of our city. Because God is in the city.

What is it like, this light traveling through our streets? How do we encounter God, who lives with us amid the smog of our cities? How do we encounter Jesus, alive and at work in the daily life of our multicultural cities?

The prophet Isaiah can guide us in this process of "learning to see." He speaks of the light which is Jesus. And now he presents Jesus to us as "Wonderful Counselor, the Mighty God, the Everlasting Father, the Prince of Peace." In this way, he introduces us to the life of the Son, so that his life can be our life.

Wonderful Counselor. The Gospels tell us how many people came up to Jesus to ask: "Master, what must we do?" The first thing that Jesus does in response is to propose, to encourage, to motivate. He keeps telling his disciples to go, to go out. He urges them to go out and meet others where they really are, not where we think they should be. Go out, again and again, go out without fear, go out without hesitation. Go out and proclaim this joy, which is for all the people.

The Mighty God. In Jesus, God himself became Emmanuel, God-with-us, the God who walks alongside us, who gets involved in our lives, in our homes, in the midst of our "pots and pans," as St. Teresa of Jesus liked to say.

The Everlasting Father. No one or anything can separate us from his love. Go out and proclaim, go out and show that God is in your midst as a merciful Father who himself goes out, morning and evening, to see if his son has returned home and, as soon as he sees him coming, runs out to embrace him. This is beautiful. An embrace which wants to take up, purify, and elevate the dignity of his children. A Father who, in his embrace, brings *glad tidings to the poor, healing to the afflicted, liberty to captives, comfort to those who mourn* (cf. Isaiah 61:1-2).

Prince of Peace. Go out to others and share the good news that God, our Father, walks at our side. He frees us from anonymity, from a life of emptiness, and brings us to the school of encounter. He removes us from the fray of competition and self-absorption, and he opens before us the path of peace. That peace which is born of accepting others, that peace which fills our hearts whenever we look upon those in need as our brothers and sisters.

God is living in our cities. The Church is living in our cities. God and the Church living in our cities want to be like yeast in the dough, to relate to everyone, to stand at everyone's side, proclaiming the marvels of the Wonderful Counselor, the Mighty God, the Eternal Father, the Prince of Peace.

"The people who walked in darkness have seen a great light." And we, as Christians, are witnesses to this.

XXIII

What about You?

Mass with Bishops, Clergy, and Religious of
Pennsylvania
Homily of Pope Francis
Cathedral of Sts. Peter and Paul, Philadelphia
Saturday, September 26, 2015

This morning I learned something about the history of this beautiful cathedral: the story behind its high walls and windows. I would like to think, though, that the history of the Church in this city and state is really a story not about building walls, but about breaking them down. It is a story about generation after generation of committed Catholics going out to the peripheries, and building communities of worship, education, charity, and service to the larger society.

That story is seen in the many shrines which dot this city and the many parish churches whose towers and steeples speak of God's presence in the midst of our communities. It is seen in the efforts of all those dedicated priests, religious, and laity who for over two centuries have ministered to the spiritual needs of the poor, the immigrant, the sick, and those in prison. And it is seen in the hundreds of schools where religious brothers and sisters trained children to read and write, to love God and neighbor, and to contribute as good citizens to the life of American society. All of this is a great legacy which you have received, and which you have been called to enrich and pass on.

Most of you know the story of St. Katharine Drexel, one of the great saints raised up by this local Church. When she spoke to Pope Leo XIII of the needs of the missions, the pope — he was a very wise pope! — asked her pointedly: "What about you? What are you going to do?" Those words changed Katharine's life, because they reminded her that, in the end, every Christian man and woman, by virtue of baptism, has received a mission. Each one of us has to respond, as best we can, to the Lord's call to build up his Body, the Church.

"What about you?" I would like to dwell on two aspects of these words in the context of our specific mission to transmit the joy of the Gospel and to build up the Church, whether as priests, deacons, or men and women who belong to institutes of consecrated life.

First, those words — "What about you?" — were addressed to a young person, a young woman with high ideals, and they changed her life. They made her think of the immense work that had to be done and to realize that she was being called to do her part. How many young people in our parishes and schools have the same high ideals, generosity of spirit, and love for Christ and the Church! I ask you: Do we challenge them? Do we make space for them and help them to do their part? To find ways of sharing their enthusiasm and gifts with our communities, above all, in works of mercy and concern for others? Do we share our own joy and enthusiasm in serving the Lord?

One of the great challenges facing the Church in this generation is to foster in all the faithful a sense of personal responsibility for the Church's mission and to enable them to fulfill that responsibility as missionary disciples, as a leaven of the Gospel in our world. This will require creativity in adapting to changed situations, carrying forward the legacy of the past not primarily by maintaining our structures and institutions, which have served us well, but above all by being open to the possibilities which the Spirit opens up to us and communicating the joy of the Gospel, daily and in every season of our life.

"What about you?" It is significant that these words of the elderly pope were also addressed to a laywoman. We know that the future of the Church in a rapidly changing society will call, and even now calls, for a much more active engagement on the part of the laity. The Church in the United States has always devoted immense effort to the work of catechesis and education. Our challenge today is to build on those solid foundations and to foster a sense of collaboration and shared responsibility in planning for the future of our parishes and institutions. This does not mean relinquishing the spiritual authority with which we have been entrusted; rather, it means discerning and employing wisely the manifold gifts which the Spirit pours out upon the Church. In a particular way, it means valuing the immense contribution which women, lay and religious, have made and continue to make in the life of our communities.

Dear brothers and sisters, I thank you for the way in which each of you has answered Jesus' question which inspired your own vocation: "What about you?" I encourage you to be renewed in the joy and wonder of that first encounter with Jesus and to draw from that joy renewed fidelity and strength. I look forward to being with you in these days and I ask you to bring my affectionate greetings to those who could not be with us, especially the many elderly priests and men and women religious who join us in spirit.

During these days of the World Meeting of Families, I would ask you in a particular way to reflect on our ministry to families, to couples preparing for marriage, and to our young people. I know how much is being done in the local Churches to respond to the needs of families and to support them in their journey of faith. I ask you to pray fervently for them and for the deliberations of the forthcoming Synod on the Family.

Now, with gratitude for all we have received, and with confident assurance in all our needs, we turn to Mary, Our Blessed Mother. With a mother's love, may she intercede for the growth of the Church in America in prophetic witness to the power of her Son's Cross to bring joy, hope, and strength into our world. I pray for each of you, and I ask you, please, to pray for me.

XXIV

ALL MEN AND WOMEN ARE CREATED EQUAL

MEETING FOR RELIGIOUS LIBERTY WITH THE HISPANIC
COMMUNITY AND OTHER IMMIGRANTS
ADDRESS OF POPE FRANCIS
INDEPENDENCE MALL, PHILADELPHIA
SATURDAY, SEPTEMBER 26, 2015

~

Dear Friends,

Good afternoon. One of the highlights of my visit is to stand
here, before Independence Hall, the birthplace of the United
States of America. It was here that the freedoms which define
this country were first proclaimed. The Declaration of Independence
stated that all men and women are created equal, that they
are endowed by their Creator with certain inalienable rights, and
that governments exist to protect and defend those rights. Those
ringing words continue to inspire us today, even as they have
inspired peoples throughout the world to fight for the freedom
to live in accordance with their dignity.

   History also shows that these or any truths must constantly
be reaffirmed, re-appropriated, and defended. The history of this
nation is also the tale of a constant effort, lasting to our own day,
to embody those lofty principles in social and political life. We
remember the great struggles which led to the abolition of slavery,
the extension of voting rights, the growth of the labor movement,
and the gradual effort to eliminate every kind of racism
and prejudice directed at further waves of new Americans. This
shows that, when a country is determined to remain true to its

principles, those founding principles based on respect for human dignity, it is strengthened and renewed. When a country is mindful of its roots, it keeps growing, it is renewed, and it continues to embrace newcomers, new individuals, and new peoples.

All of us benefit from remembering our past. A people which remembers does not repeat past errors; instead, it looks with confidence to the challenges of the present and the future. Remembrance saves a people's soul from whatever or whoever would attempt to dominate it or to use it for their own interests. When individuals and communities are guaranteed the effective exercise of their rights, they are not only free to realize their potential, they also, through their talents and their hard work, contribute to the welfare and enrichment of society as a whole.

In this place which is symbolic of the American way, I would like to reflect with you on the right to religious freedom. It is a fundamental right which shapes the way we interact socially and personally with our neighbors whose religious views differ from our own, the ideal of interreligious dialogue, where all men and women, from different religious traditions, can speak to one another without arguing. This is what religious freedom allows.

Religious freedom certainly means the right to worship God, individually and in community, as our consciences dictate. But religious liberty, by its nature, transcends places of worship and the private sphere of individuals and families. Because religion itself, the religious dimension, is not a subculture; it is part of the culture of every people and every nation.

Our various religious traditions serve society primarily by the message they proclaim. They call individuals and communities to worship God, the source of all life, liberty, and happiness. They remind us of the transcendent dimension of human existence and our irreducible freedom in the face of any claim to absolute power. We need but look at history — we always benefit from looking at history — especially the history of the last century, to see the atrocities perpetrated by systems which claimed to build one or another "earthly paradise" by dominating peoples, subjecting them to apparently indisputable principles, and denying them any kind of rights. Our rich religious traditions seek to offer meaning and direction, "they have an enduring power to open new horizons, to stimulate thought, to expand the mind and heart" (*Evangelii Gaudium*, 256). They call to conversion, reconciliation, concern for the future of society, self-sacrifice in the service of the common good, and compassion for those in need. At the heart of their spiritual mission is the proclamation of the truth and dignity of the human person and all human rights.

Our religious traditions remind us that, as human beings, we are called to acknowledge an Other who reveals our relational identity in the face of every effort to impose "a uniformity to which the egotism of the powerful, the conformism of the weak, or the ideology of the utopian would seek to impose on us" (M. de Certeau).

In a world where various forms of modern tyranny seek to suppress religious freedom, or, as I said earlier, to try to reduce it to a subculture without right to a voice in the public square, or to use religion as a pretext for hatred and brutality, it is imperative that the followers of the various religious traditions join their voices in calling for peace, tolerance, and respect for the dignity and the rights of others.

We live in an age subject to the "globalization of the technocratic paradigm" (*Laudato Si'*, 106), which consciously aims at a one-dimensional uniformity and seeks to eliminate all differences and traditions in a superficial quest for unity. The religions thus have the right and the duty to make clear that it is possible to build a society where "a healthy pluralism ... which genuinely respects differences and values them as such" (*Evangelii Gaudium*, 255) is a precious ally "in the commitment to defending human dignity ... and a path to peace in our troubled world," wounded as it is by wars (ibid., 257).

The Quakers who founded Philadelphia were inspired by a profound evangelical sense of the dignity of each individual and the ideal of a community united by brotherly love. This conviction led them to found a colony which would be a haven of religious freedom and tolerance. That sense of fraternal concern for the dignity of all, especially the weak and the vulnerable, became an essential part of the American spirit. During his visit to the United States in 1987, St. John Paul II paid moving homage to this, reminding all Americans that: "The ultimate test of your greatness is the way you treat every human being, but especially the weakest and most defenseless ones" (*Farewell Address*, September 19, 1987, 3).

I take this opportunity to thank all those, of whatever religion, who have sought to serve God, the God of peace, by building cities of brotherly love, by caring for our neighbors in need, by defending the dignity of God's gift, the gift of life in all its stages, and by defending the cause of the poor and the immigrant. All too often, those most in need of our help, everywhere, are unable to be heard. You are their voice, and many of you — men and women — have faithfully made their cry heard. In this witness, which frequently encounters powerful resistance, you remind American democracy of the ideals for which it was founded, and that society is weakened whenever and wherever injustice prevails.

Just now I spoke of the trend towards globalization. Globalization is not evil. On the contrary, the tendency to become globalized is good; it brings us together. What can be evil is how it happens. If a certain kind of globalization claims to make everyone uniform, to level everyone out, that globalization destroys the rich gifts and uniqueness of each person and each people. But a globalization which attempts to bring everyone together while respecting the uniqueness and gifts of each person or people is a good globalization; it helps all of us to grow, and it brings peace. I like to use a geometrical image for this. If globalization is a sphere, where every point is equidistant from the center, it cancels everything out; it is not good. But if globalization is like a polyhedron, where everything is united but each element keeps its own identity, then it is good; it causes a people to grow, it bestows dignity, and it grants rights to all.

Among us today are members of America's large Hispanic population, as well as representatives of recent immigrants to the United States. Many of you have emigrated (I greet you warmly!) to this country, at great personal cost, in the hope of building a new life. Do not be discouraged by whatever hardships you face. I ask you not to forget that, like those who came here before you, you bring many gifts to this nation. Please, you should never be ashamed of your traditions. Do not forget the lessons you learned from your elders, which are something you can bring to enrich the life of this American land.

I repeat, do not be ashamed of what is part of you, your life blood. You are also called to be responsible citizens and to contribute fruitfully — as those who came before you did with such fortitude — to the life of the communities in which you live. I think in particular of the vibrant faith which so many of you possess, the deep sense of family life and all those other values which you have inherited. By contributing your gifts, you will not only find your place here, you will help to renew society from within. Do not forget what took place here over two centuries ago. Do not forget that Declaration which proclaimed that all men and women are created equal, that they are endowed by their Creator with certain inalienable rights, and that governments exist in order to protect and defend those rights.

Dear friends, I thank you for your warm welcome and for joining me here today. Let us preserve freedom. Let us cherish freedom. Freedom of conscience, religious freedom, the freedom of each person, each family, each people, which is what gives rise to rights. May this country and each of you be renewed in gratitude for the many blessings and freedoms that you enjoy. And may you defend these rights, especially your religious freedom, for it has been given to you by God himself. May he bless you all. I ask you, please, say a little prayer for me. Thank you.

XXV

THE FAMILY, A WORKSHOP OF HOPE

PRAYER VIGIL FOR THE FESTIVAL OF FAMILIES
ADDRESS OF POPE FRANCIS
BENJAMIN FRANKLIN PARKWAY, PHILADELPHIA
SATURDAY, SEPTEMBER 26, 2015

~

Dear Brothers and Sisters,
Dear Families,

I thank those who offered their witness and those who brought us joy through their art, through beauty, which is the way to God. Beauty brings us to God. And a truthful witness brings us to God, because God is also truth. He is beauty, and he is truth. A witness intended to help others is good, it makes us good, because God is goodness. It brings us to God. All that is good, all that is true, and all that is beautiful brings us to God. Because God is good, God is beauty, God is truth.

I thank all of you. Those who spoke to us and the presence of everyone here [is] itself a witness, a truthful witness that family life is something worthwhile, and that a society grows stronger and better, it grows in beauty and it grows in truth, when it rises on the foundation of the family.

A young person once asked me — you know how young people ask hard questions! — "Father, what did God do before he created the world?" Believe me, I had a hard time answering that one. I told him what I am going to tell you now. Before he created the world, God was in love, because God is love. The love he had within himself, the love between the Father and the Son, in the Holy Spirit, was so great, so overflowing — I'm not sure if this is theologically precise, but you will get what I am saying — that love was so great that God could not be selfish. He had to go out from himself, in order to have someone to love outside of himself. So God created the world. God made this wonderful world in which we live and which, since we are not too smart, we are now in the process of destroying. But the most beautiful thing God made — so the Bible tells us — was the family. He created man and woman. And he gave them everything. He entrusted the world to them: "Grow, multiply, cultivate the earth, make it bear fruit, let it grow." All the love he put into that marvelous creation, he entrusted to a family.

Let's go back a bit. All the love God has in himself, all the beauty God has in himself, all the truth God has in himself, he entrusts to the family. A family is truly a family when it is capable of opening its arms to receive all that love. Of course, the Garden of Eden is long gone; life has its problems; men and women — through the wiles of the devil — experienced division. And all that love which God gave us was practically lost. And in no time, the first crime was committed, the first fratricide. Brother kills brother: war. God's love, beauty, and truth, and on the other hand the destructiveness of war: we are poised between those two realities even today. It is up to us to choose, to decide which way to go.

But let's go back. When the man and his wife went astray and walked away from God, God did not leave them alone. Such was his love. So great was his love that he began to walk with mankind, he began to walk alongside his people, until the right time came, and then he gave the greatest demonstration of love: his Son. And where did he send his Son? To a palace, to a city, to an office building? He sent him to a family. God came into the world in a family. And he could do this because that family was a family with a heart open to love, a family whose doors were open.

We can think of Mary, a young woman. She couldn't believe it: "How can this be?" But once it was explained to her, she obeyed. We think of Joseph, full of dreams for making a home;

then along comes this surprise which he doesn't understand. He accepts; he obeys. And in the loving obedience of this woman, Mary, and this man, Joseph, we have a family into which God comes. God always knocks on the doors of our hearts. He likes to do that. He goes out from within. But do you know what he likes best of all? To knock on the doors of families. And to see families which are united, families which love, families which bring up their children, educating them and helping them to grow, families which build a society of goodness, truth, and beauty.

We are celebrating the festival of families. The family has a divine identity card. Do you see what I mean? God gave the family an identity card, so that families could be places in our world where his truth, love, and beauty could continue to take root and grow. Some of you may say to me: "Father, you can say that because you're not married!" Certainly, in the family there are difficulties. In families we argue. In families sometimes we throw dishes. In families children cause headaches. I'm not going to say anything about mothers-in-law! Families always, always, have crosses. Always. Because the love of God, the Son of God, also asked us to follow him along this way. But in families also, the cross is followed by resurrection, because there too the Son of God leads us.

So the family is — if you excuse the word — a workshop of hope, of the hope of life and resurrection, since God was the one who opened this path. Then too, there are children. Children are hard work. When we were children, we were hard work. Sometimes back home I see some of my staff who come to work with rings under their eyes. They have a one- or two-month-old baby. And I ask them: "Didn't you get any sleep?" And they say: "No, the baby cried all night." In families, there are difficulties, but those difficulties are resolved by love. Hatred doesn't resolve any difficulty. Divided hearts do not resolve difficulties. Only love is capable of resolving difficulty. Love is a celebration, love is joy, love is perseverance.

I don't want to keep on talking because it will go on too long, but I did want to stress two little points about the family. I would ask you to think about them. We have to care in a special way for children and for grandparents. Children and young people are the future; they are our strength; they are what keep us moving forward. They are the ones in whom we put our hope. Grandparents are a family's memory. They are the ones who gave us the faith, they passed the faith on to us. Taking care of grandparents and taking care of children is the sign of love — I'm not sure if it is the greatest, but for the family I would say that it is the most promising — because it promises the future. A people incapable of caring for children and caring for the elderly is a people without a future, because it lacks the strength and the memory needed to move forward.

The family is beautiful, but it takes hard work; it brings problems. In the family, sometimes there is fighting. The husband argues with the wife; they get upset with each other, or children get upset with their parents. May I offer a bit of advice: never end the day without making peace in the family. In the family the day cannot end in fighting. May God bless you. May God give you strength. May God inspire you to keep moving forward. Let us care for the family. Let us defend the family, because there our future is at stake. Thank you. God bless you, and please pray for me.

Dear Brothers and Sisters,
Dear Families,

First of all, I want to thank the families who were willing to share their life stories with us. Thank you for your witness! It is always a gift to listen to families share their life experiences; it touches our hearts. We feel that they speak to us about things that are very personal and unique, which in some way involve all of us. In listening to their experiences, we can feel ourselves drawn in, challenged as married couples and parents, as children, brothers and sisters, and grandparents.

As I was listening, I was thinking how important it is for us to share our home life and to help one another in this marvelous and challenging task of "being a family."

Being with you makes me think of one of the most beautiful mysteries of our Christian faith. God did not want to come into the world other than through a family. God did not want to draw near to humanity other than through a home. God did not want any other name for himself than Emmanuel (cf. Matthew 1:23). He is "God with us." This was his desire from the beginning, his purpose, his constant effort: to say to us: "I am God with you, I am God for you." He is the God who from the very beginning of creation said: *It is not good for man to be alone* (cf. Genesis 2:18). We can add: it is not good for woman to be alone, it is not good for children, the elderly or the young to be alone. It is not good. That is why a man leaves his father and mother, and clings to his wife, and the two of them become one flesh (cf. Genesis 2:24). The two are meant to be a home, a family.

From time immemorial, in the depths of our heart, we have heard those powerful words: it is not good for you to be alone. The family is the great blessing, the great gift of this "God with us," who did not want to abandon us to the solitude of a life without others, without challenges, without a home.

God does not dream by himself, he tries to do everything "with us." His dream constantly comes true in the dreams of many couples who work to make their life that of a family. That is why the family is the living symbol of the loving plan of which the Father once dreamed. To want to form a family is to resolve to be a part of God's dream, to choose to dream with him, to want to build with him, to join him in this saga of building a world where no one will feel alone, unwanted, or homeless.

As Christians, we appreciate the beauty of the family and of family life as the place where we come to learn the meaning and value of human relationships. We learn that "to love someone is not just a strong feeling — it is a decision, it is a judgment, it is a promise" (Erich Fromm, *The Art of Loving*). We learn to stake everything on another person, and we learn that it is worth it.

Jesus was not a confirmed bachelor, far from it! He took the Church as his bride, and made her a people of his own. He laid down his life for those he loved, so that his bride, the Church, could always know that he is God with us, his people, his family. We cannot understand Christ without his Church, just as we cannot understand the Church without her spouse, Christ Jesus, who gave his life out of love, and who makes us see that it is worth the price.

Laying down one's life out of love is not easy. As with the Master, "staking everything" can sometimes involve the cross, times when everything seems uphill. I think of all those parents, all those families who lack employment or workers' rights, and how this is a true cross. How many sacrifices they make to earn their daily bread! It is understandable that, when these parents return home, they are so weary that they cannot give their best to their children.

I think of all those families which lack housing or live in overcrowded conditions. Families which lack the basics to be able to build bonds of closeness, security, and protection from troubles of any kind.

I think of all those families which lack access to basic health services. Families which, when faced with medical problems, especially those of their younger or older members, are dependent on a system which fails to meet their needs, is insensitive to their pain, and forces them to make great sacrifices to receive adequate treatment.

We cannot call any society healthy when it does not leave real room for family life. We cannot think that a society has a future when it fails to pass laws capable of protecting families and ensuring their basic needs, especially those of families just starting out. How many problems would be solved if our societies protected families and provided households, especially those of recently married couples, with the possibility of dignified work, housing and health care services to accompany them throughout life.

God's dream does not change; it remains intact and invites us to work for a society which supports families. A society where bread, "fruit of the earth and the work of human hands," continues to be put on the table of every home, to nourish the hope of its children.

Let us help one another to make it possible to "stake everything on love." Let us help one another at times of difficulty and lighten each other's burdens. Let us support one another. Let us be families which are a support for other families.

Perfect families do not exist. This must not discourage us. Quite the opposite. Love is something we learn; love is something we live; love grows as it is "forged" by the concrete situations which each particular family experiences. Love is born and constantly develops amid lights and shadows. Love can flourish in men and women who try not to make conflict the last word, but rather a new opportunity — an opportunity to seek help, an opportunity to question how we need to improve, an opportunity to discover the God who is with us and never abandons us. This is a great legacy that we can give to our children, a very good lesson: we make mistakes, yes; we have problems, yes. But we know that that is not really what counts. We know that mistakes, problems, and conflicts are an opportunity to draw closer to others, to draw closer to God.

This evening we have come together to pray, to pray as a family, to make our homes the joyful face of the Church. To meet that God who did not want to come into our world in any other way than through a family. To meet "God with us," the God who is always in our midst.

XXVI

I Humbly Beg You

MEETING WITH VICTIMS OF SEXUAL ABUSE
ADDRESS OF POPE FRANCIS
ST. CHARLES BORROMEO SEMINARY, PHILADELPHIA
SUNDAY, SEPTEMBER 27, 2015

~

My dearest brothers and sisters in Christ, I am grateful for this opportunity to meet you. I am blessed by your presence. Thank you for corning here today.

Words cannot fully express my sorrow for the abuse you suffered. You are precious children of God who should always expect our protection, our care, and our love. I am profoundly sorry that your innocence was violated by those who you trusted. In some cases the trust was betrayed by members of your own family, in other cases by priests who carry a sacred responsibility for the care of souls. In all circumstances, the betrayal was a terrible violation of human dignity.

For those who were abused by a member of the clergy, I am deeply sorry for the times when you or your family spoke out, to report the abuse, but you were not heard or believed. Please know that the Holy Father hears you and believes you. I deeply regret that some bishops failed in their responsibility to protect children. It is very disturbing to know that in some cases bishops even were abusers. I pledge to you that we will follow the path of truth wherever it may lead. Clergy and bishops will be held accountable when they abuse or fail to protect children.

We are gathered here in Philadelphia to celebrate God's gift of family life. Within our family of faith and our human families, the sins and crimes of sexual abuse of children must no longer be held in secret and in shame. As we anticipate the Jubilee Year of

Mercy, your presence, so generously given despite the anger and pain you have experienced, reveals the merciful heart of Christ. Your stories of survival, each unique and compelling, are powerful signs of the hope that comes from the Lord's promise to be with us always.

It is good to know that you have brought family members and friends with you today. I am grateful for their compassionate support and pray that many people of the Church will respond to the call to accompany those who have suffered abuse. May the Door of Mercy be opened wide in our dioceses, our parishes, our homes and our hearts, to receive those who were abused and to seek the path to forgiveness by trusting in the Lord. We promise to support your continued healing and to always be vigilant to protect the children of today and tomorrow.

When the disciples who walked with Jesus on the road to Emmaus recognized that he was the risen Lord, they asked Jesus to stay with them. Like those disciples, I humbly beg you and all survivors of abuse to stay with us, to stay with the Church, and that together, as pilgrims on the journey of faith, we might find our way to the Father.

XXVII

A Renewed Closeness between the Family and the Church

Meeting with the Bishops Taking Part in the
World Meeting of Families
Address of Pope Francis
St. Charles Borromeo Seminary,
Chapel of St. Martin, Philadelphia
Sunday, September 27, 2015

~

Dear Brother Bishops,

Good morning. I am deeply pained by the stories, the sufferings, and the pain of minors who were sexually abused by priests. I continue to be ashamed that persons charged with the tender care of those little ones abused them and caused them grave harm. I deeply regret this. God weeps. The crimes and sins of sexual abuse of minors may no longer be kept secret; I commit myself to ensuring that the Church makes every effort to protect minors, and I promise that those responsible will be held to account. Survivors of abuse have become true heralds of hope and ministers of mercy; humbly we owe our gratitude to each of them and to their families for their great courage in shedding the light of Christ on the evil sexual abuse of minors. I say this because I have just met with a group of persons abused as children, who are helped and accompanied here in Philadelphia with particular care by Archbishop [Charles] Chaput, and we felt that I should communicate this to you.

I am happy to be able to share these moments of pastoral reflection with you, amid the joyful celebrations for the World Meeting of Families. I am speaking in Spanish because they told me that you all know Spanish.

For the Church, the family is not first and foremost a cause for concern, but rather the joyous confirmation of God's blessing upon the masterpiece of creation. Every day, all over the world, the Church can rejoice in the Lord's gift of so many families who, even amid difficult trials, remain faithful to their promises and keep the faith!

I would say that the foremost pastoral challenge of our changing times is to move decisively towards recognizing this gift. For all the obstacles we see before us, gratitude and appreciation should prevail over concerns and complaints. The family is the fundamental locus of the covenant between the Church and God's creation, with that creation which God blessed on the last day with a family. Without the family, not even the Church would exist. Nor could she be what she is called to be, namely, "a sign and instrument" of communion with God "and of the unity of the whole human race" (*Lumen Gentium*, 1).

Needless to say, our understanding, shaped by the interplay of ecclesial faith and the conjugal experience of sacramental grace, must not lead us to disregard the unprecedented changes taking place in contemporary society, with their social, cultural — and, sadly, also legal — effects on family bonds. These changes affect all of us, believers and nonbelievers alike. Christians are not "immune" to the changes of their times. This concrete world, with all its many problems and possibilities, is where we must live, believe. and proclaim.

Until recently, we lived in a social context where the similarities between the civil institution of marriage and the Christian sacrament were considerable and shared. The two were interrelated and mutually supportive. This is no longer the case. To describe our situation today, I would use two familiar images: our neighborhood stores and our large supermarkets.

There was a time when one neighborhood store had everything one needed for personal and family life. The products may not have been cleverly displayed, or offered much choice, but there was a personal bond between the shopkeeper and his customers. Business was done on the basis of trust, people knew one another; they were all neighbors. They trusted one another. They built up trust. These stores were often simply known as "the local market."

Then a different kind of store grew up: the supermarket. Huge spaces with a great selection of merchandise. The world seems to have become one of these great supermarkets; our culture has become more and more competitive. Business is no longer conducted on the basis of trust; others can no longer be trusted. There are no longer close personal relationships. Today's culture seems to encourage people not to bond with anything or anyone, not to trust.

The most important thing nowadays seems to be to follow the latest trend or activity. This is even true of religion. Today, consumption seems to determine what is important. Consuming relationships, consuming friendships, consuming religions, consuming, consuming … whatever the cost or consequences, a consumption which does not favor bonding, a consumption which has little to do with human relationships. Social bonds are a mere "means" for the satisfaction of "my needs." The important thing is no longer our neighbor, with his or her familiar face, story, and personality.

The result is a culture which discards everything that is no longer "useful" or "satisfying" for the tastes of the consumer. We have turned our society into a huge multicultural showcase tied only to the tastes of certain "consumers," while so many others only "eat the crumbs that fall from their master's table" (Matthew 15:27).

This causes great harm; it greatly wounds our culture. I daresay that at the root of so many contemporary situations is a kind of impoverishment born of a widespread and radical sense of loneliness. Running after the latest fad, accumulating "friends" on one of the social networks, we get caught up in what contemporary society has to offer, loneliness with fear of commitment in a limitless effort to feel recognized.

Should we blame our young people for having grown up in this kind of society? Should we condemn them for living in this kind of a world? Should they hear their pastors saying that "it was all better back then," "the world is falling apart and if things go on this way, who knows where we will end up?" It makes me think of an Argentine tango! No, I do not think that this is the way. As shepherds following in the footsteps of the Good Shepherd, we are asked to seek out, to accompany, to lift up, to bind up the wounds of our time. To look at things realistically, with the eyes of one who feels called to action, to pastoral conversion. The world today demands this pastoral conversion on our part. "It is vitally important for the Church today to go forth and preach the Gospel to all: to all places, on all occasions, without hesitation, reluctance or fear. The joy of the Gospel is for all people: no one can be excluded" (*Evangelii Gaudium*, 23). The Gospel is not a product to be consumed; it is not a part of this culture of consumption.

We would be mistaken, however, to see this "culture" of the present world as mere indifference towards marriage and the family, as pure and simple selfishness. Are today's young people hopelessly timid, weak, inconsistent? We must not fall into this trap. Many young people, in the context of this culture of discouragement, have yielded to a form of unconscious acquiescence. They are afraid, deep down, paralyzed before the beautiful, noble, and truly necessary challenges. Many put off marriage while waiting for ideal conditions, when everything can be perfect. Meanwhile, life goes on, without really being lived to the full. For knowledge of life's true pleasures only comes as the fruit of a long-term, generous investment of our intelligence, enthusiasm, and passion.

Addressing Congress a few days ago, I said that we are living in a culture which pressures some young people not to start a family because they lack the material means to do so, and others because they are so well off that they are happy as they are. That is the temptation, not to start a family.

As pastors, we bishops are called to collect our energies and to rebuild enthusiasm for making families correspond ever more fully to the blessing of God which they are! We need to invest our energies not so much in rehearsing the problems of the world around us and the merits of Christianity, but in extending a sincere invitation to young people to be brave and to opt for marriage and the family. In Buenos Aires, many women used to complain about their children who were thirty, thirty-two, or thirty-four years old and still single: "I don't know what to do" — "Well, stop ironing their shirts!" Young people have to be encouraged to take this risk, but it is a risk of fruitfulness and life.

Here too, we need a bit of holy *parrhesia* on the part of bishops. "Why aren't you married?" "Yes, I have a fiancée, but we don't know ... maybe yes, maybe no ... We're saving some money for the party, for this or that ..." The holy *parrhesia* to accompany them and make them grow towards the commitment of marriage.

A Christianity which "does" little in practice, while incessantly "explaining" its teachings, is dangerously unbalanced. I would even say that it is stuck in a vicious circle. A pastor must show that the "Gospel of the family" is truly "good news" in a world where self-concern seems to reign supreme! We are not speaking about some romantic dream: the perseverance which is called for in having a family and raising it transforms the world and human history. Families transform the world and history.

A pastor serenely yet passionately proclaims the word of God. He encourages believers to aim high. He will enable his brothers and sisters to hear and experience God's promise, which can expand their experience of motherhood and fatherhood within the horizon of a new "familiarity" with God (Mark 3:31-35).

A pastor watches over the dreams, the lives and the growth of his flock. This "watchfulness" is not the result of talking but of shepherding. Only one capable of standing "in the midst of" the flock can be watchful, not someone who is afraid of questions, afraid of contact and accompaniment. A pastor keeps watch first and foremost with prayer, supporting the faith of his people and instilling confidence in the Lord, in his presence. A pastor remains vigilant by helping people to lift their gaze at times of discouragement, frustration, and failure. We might well ask whether in our pastoral ministry we are ready to "waste" time with families. Whether we are ready to be present to them, sharing their difficulties and joys.

Naturally, experiencing the spirit of this joyful familiarity with God, and then spreading its powerful evangelical fruitfulness, has to be the primary feature of our lifestyle as bishops: a lifestyle of prayer and preaching the Gospel (Acts of the Apostles 6:4). I have always been struck by how, in the early days of the Church, the Hellenists complained that their widows and orphans were not being well cared for. The apostles, of course, weren't able to handle this themselves, so they got together and came up with deacons. The Holy Spirit inspired them to create deacons, and when Peter announced the decision, he explained, "We are going to choose seven men to take care of this; for our part, we have two responsibilities: prayer and preaching." What is the first job of bishops? To pray. The second job goes along with this: to preach. We are helped by this dogmatic definition. Unless I am wrong, Cardinal [Gerhard] Müller helps us because he defines what is the role of the bishop. The bishop is charged to be a pastor, but to be a pastor first and foremost by his prayer and preaching, because everything else follows, if there is time.

By our own humble Christian apprenticeship in the familial virtues of God's people, we will become more and more like fathers and mothers (as did St. Paul: cf. 1 Thessalonians 2:7,11), and less like people who have simply learned to live without a family. Lack of contact with families makes us people who learn to live without a family, and this is not good. Our ideal is not to live without love! A good pastor renounces the love of a family precisely in order to focus all his energies, and the grace of his particular vocation, on the evangelical blessing of the love of men and women who carry forward God's plan of creation, beginning with those who are lost, abandoned, wounded, broken, downtrodden, and deprived of their dignity. This total surrender to God's *agape* is certainly not a vocation lacking in tenderness and affection! We need but look to Jesus to understand this (cf. Matthew 19:12). The mission of a good pastor, in the style of God

— and only God can authorize this, not our own presumption! — imitates in every way and for all people the Son's love for the Father. This is reflected in the tenderness with which a pastor devotes himself to the loving care of the men and women of our human family.

For the eyes of faith, this is a most valuable sign. Our ministry needs to deepen the covenant between the Church and the family. I repeat this: to deepen the covenant between the Church and the family. Otherwise it becomes arid, and the human family will grow irremediably distant, by our own fault, from God's joyful good news, and will go to the latest supermarket to buy whatever product suits them then and there.

If we prove capable of the demanding task of reflecting God's love, cultivating infinite patience and serenity as we strive to sow its seeds in the frequently crooked furrows in which we are called to plant — for very often we really do have to sow in crooked furrows — then even a Samaritan woman with five "non-husbands" will discover that she is capable of giving witness. And for every rich young man who with sadness feels that he has to calmly keep considering the matter, an older publican will come down from the tree and give fourfold to the poor, to whom, before that moment, he had never even given a thought.

My brothers, may God grant us this gift of a renewed closeness between the family and the Church. Families need it, the Church needs it, and we pastors need it.

The family is our ally, our window to the world; the family is the proof of an irrevocable blessing of God destined for all the children who in every age are born into this difficult yet beautiful creation which God has asked us to serve! Thank you.

XXVIII

Jesus Saves Us from the Lie That Says No One Can Change

Visit to Detainees at Curran-Fromhold Correctional Facility, Philadelphia
Address of Pope Francis
Sunday, September 27, 2015

~

Dear Brothers and Sisters,

Good morning. I am going to speak in Spanish because I don't speak English, but he [pointing to the interpreter] speaks good English, and he is going to translate for me. Thank you for receiving me and giving me the opportunity to be here with you and to share this time in your lives. It is a difficult time, one full of struggles. I know it is a painful time not only for you, but also for your families and for all of society. Any society, any family, which cannot share or take seriously the pain of its children, and views that pain as something normal or to be expected, is a society "condemned" to remain a hostage to itself, prey to the very things which cause that pain.

I am here as a pastor, but above all as a brother, to share your situation and to make it my own. I have come so that we can pray together and offer our God everything that causes us pain, but also everything that gives us hope, so that we can receive from him the power of the Resurrection.

I think of the Gospel scene where Jesus washes the feet of his disciples at the Last Supper. This was something his disciples found hard to accept. Even Peter refused, and told him, "You shall never wash my feet" (John 13:8).

In those days, it was the custom to wash someone's feet when they came to your home. That was how they welcomed people. The roads were not paved, they were covered with dust, and little stones would get stuck in your sandals. Everyone walked those roads, which left their feet dusty, bruised, or cut from those stones. That is why we see Jesus washing feet, our feet, the feet of his disciples, then and now.

We all know that life is a journey, along different roads, different paths, which leave their mark on us.

We also know in faith that Jesus seeks us out. He wants to heal our wounds, to soothe our feet which hurt from traveling alone, to wash each of us clean of the dust from our journey. He doesn't ask us where we have been; he doesn't question us about we have done. Rather, he tells us, *Unless I wash your feet, you have no share with me* (cf. John 13:8). Unless I wash your feet, I will not be able to give you the life which the Father always dreamed of, the life for which he created you. Jesus comes to meet us, so that he can restore our dignity as children of God. He wants to help us to set out again, to resume our journey, to recover our hope, to restore our faith and trust. He wants us to keep walking along the paths of life, to realize that we have a mission, and that confinement is never the same thing as exclusion.

Life means "getting our feet dirty" from the dust-filled roads of life and history. All of us need to be cleansed, to be washed. All of us. Myself, first and foremost. All of us are being sought out by the Teacher, who wants to help us resume our journey. The Lord goes in search of us; to all of us he stretches out a helping hand.

It is painful when we see prison systems which are not concerned to care for wounds, to soothe pain, to offer new possibilities. It is painful when we see people who think that only others need to be cleansed, purified, and do not recognize that their weariness, pain, and wounds are also the weariness, pain, and wounds of society. The Lord tells us this clearly with a sign: he washes our feet so we can come back to the table. The table from which he wishes no one to be excluded. The table which is spread for all and to which all of us are invited.

This time in your life can only have one purpose: to give you a hand in getting back on the right road, to give you a hand to help you rejoin society. All of us are part of that effort, all of us are invited to encourage, help, and enable your rehabilitation. A rehabilitation which everyone seeks and desires: inmates and their families, correctional authorities, social and educational programs. A rehabilitation which benefits and elevates the morale of the entire community and society.

I encourage you to have this attitude with one another and with all those who in any way are part of this institution. May you make possible new opportunities; may you blaze new trails, new paths. All of us have something we need to be cleansed of, or purified from. All of us. May the knowledge of this fact inspire us all to live in solidarity, to support one another and seek the best for others.

Let us look to Jesus, who washes our feet. He is "the way, and the truth, and the life." He comes to save us from the lie that says no one can change, the lie of thinking that no one can change. Jesus helps us to journey along the paths of life and fulfillment. May the power of his love and his resurrection always be a path leading you to new life.

Just as we are, seated, let us silently ask the Lord to bless us. May the Lord bless you and keep you. May he make his face shine upon you and be gracious to you. May he lift up his countenance upon you and give you peace. Thank you.

Impromptu Comments at the End of the Meeting:

The chair you made is very nice, very beautiful. Thanks for your work.

XXIX

Holiness Is Always Tied to Little Gestures

Closing Mass of the Eighth World Meeting
of Families
Homily of Pope Francis
Benjamin Franklin Parkway, Philadelphia
Sunday, September 27, 2015

Today the word of God surprises us with powerful and thought-provoking images. Images which challenge us, but also stir our enthusiasm.

In the first reading, Joshua tells Moses that two members of the people are prophesying, speaking God's word, without a mandate. In the Gospel, John tells Jesus that the disciples had stopped someone from casting out evil spirits in the name of Jesus. Here is the surprise: Moses and Jesus both rebuke those closest to them for being so narrow! Would that all could be prophets of God's word! Would that everyone could work miracles in the Lord's name!

Jesus encountered hostility from people who did not accept what he said and did. For them, his openness to the honest and sincere faith of many men and women who were not part of God's chosen people seemed intolerable. The disciples, for their part, acted in good faith. But the temptation to be scandalized by the freedom of God, who sends rain on the righteous and the unrighteous alike (Matthew 5:45), bypassing bureaucracy, officialdom, and inner circles, threatens the authenticity of faith. Hence it must be vigorously rejected. Once we realize this, we can understand why Jesus' words about causing "scandal" are so harsh. For Jesus, the truly "intolerable" scandal is everything that breaks down and destroys our trust in the working of the Spirit!

Our Father will not be outdone in generosity, and he continues to scatter seeds. He scatters the seeds of his presence in our world, for *love consists in this, not that we have loved God but that he loved us first* (cf. 1 John 4:10). That love gives us the profound certainty that we are sought by God; he waits for us. It is this confidence which makes disciples encourage, support, and nurture the good things happening all around them. God wants all his children to take part in the feast of the Gospel. Jesus says, "Do not hold back anything that is good, instead, help it to grow!" To raise doubts about the working of the Spirit, to give the impression that it cannot take place in those who are not "part of our group," who are not "like us," is a dangerous temptation. Not only does it block conversion to the faith, it is a perversion of faith!

Faith opens a "window" to the presence and working of the Spirit. It shows us that, like happiness, holiness is always tied to little gestures. *Whoever gives you a cup of water in my name will not go unrewarded*, says Jesus (cf. Mark 9:41). These little gestures are those we learn at home, in the family; they get lost amid all the other things we do, yet they do make each day different. They are the quiet things done by mothers and grandmothers, by fathers and grandfathers, by children, by brothers and sisters. They are little signs of tenderness, affection, and compassion. Like the warm supper we look forward to at night, the early lunch awaiting someone who gets up early to go to work. "Homey" gestures. Like a blessing before we go to bed, or a hug after we return from a hard day's work. Love is shown by little things, by attention to small daily signs which make us feel at home. Faith grows when it is lived and shaped by love. That is why our families, our homes, are true domestic churches. They are the right place for faith to become life, and life to grow in faith.

Jesus tells us not to hold back these little miracles. Instead, he wants us to encourage them, to spread them. He asks us to go through life, our everyday life, encouraging all these little signs of love as signs of his own living and active presence in our world.

So we might ask ourselves, today, here, at the conclusion of this meeting: How are we trying to live this way in our homes, in our societies? What kind of world do we want to leave to our children (cf. *Laudato Si'*, 160)? We cannot answer these questions alone, by ourselves. It is the Spirit who challenges us to respond as part of the great human family. Our common house can no longer tolerate sterile divisions. The urgent challenge of protecting our home includes the effort to bring the entire human family together in the pursuit of a sustainable and integral development, for we know that things can change (cf. ibid., 13). May our children find in us models and incentives to communion, not division! May our children find in us men and women capable of joining others in bringing to full flower all the good seeds which the Father has sown!

Pointedly, yet affectionately, Jesus tells us: "If you then, who are evil, know how to give good gifts to your children, how much more will the heavenly Father give the Holy Spirit to those who ask him!" (Luke 11:13). How much wisdom there is in these few words! It is true that, as far as goodness and purity of heart are concerned, we human beings don't have much to show! But Jesus knows that, where children are concerned, we are capable of boundless generosity. So he reassures us: if only we have faith, the Father will give us his Spirit.

We Christians, the Lord's disciples, ask the families of the world to help us! How many of us are here at this celebration! This is itself something prophetic, a kind of miracle in today's world, which is tired of inventing new divisions, new hurts, new disasters. Would that we could all be prophets! Would that all of us could be open to miracles of love to benefit our own families and all the families of the world, and thus overcome the scandal of a narrow, petty love, closed in on itself, impatient of others! I leave you with a question for each of you to answer — because I said the word "impatient": At home do we shout at one another or do we speak with love and tenderness? This is a good way of measuring our love.

And how beautiful it would be if everywhere, even beyond our borders, we could appreciate and encourage this prophecy and this miracle! We renew our faith in the word of the Lord which invites faithful families to this openness. It invites all those who want to share the prophecy of the covenant of man and woman, which generates life and reveals God! May the Lord help us to be sharers in the prophecy of peace, of tenderness and affection in the family. May his word help us to share in the prophetic sign of watching over our children and our grandparents with tenderness, with patience, and with love.

Anyone who wants to bring into this world a family which teaches children to be excited by every gesture aimed at overcoming evil — a family which shows that the Spirit is alive and at work — will encounter our gratitude and our appreciation. Whatever the family, people, religion, or region to which they belong!

May God grant that all of us may be prophets of the joy of the Gospel, the Gospel of the family and family love, as disciples of the Lord. May he grant us the grace to be worthy of that purity of heart which is not scandalized by the Gospel! Amen.

XXX

Jesus Is in Your Midst

Greeting to the Organizers, Volunteers, and
Benefactors of the World Meeting of Families
Address of Pope Francis
Philadelphia International Airport
Sunday, September 27, 2015

~

Dear Friends,

My days with you have been brief. But they have been days of great grace for me and, I pray, for you too. Please know that as I prepare to leave, I do so with a heart full of gratitude and hope.

I am grateful to all of you and to the many others who worked so hard to make my visit possible and to prepare for the World Meeting of Families. In a particular way I thank the Archdiocese of Philadelphia, the civil authorities, the organizers, and all the many volunteers and benefactors who assisted in ways large and small.

I also thank the families who shared their witness during the Meeting. It is not so easy to speak openly of one's life journey! But their honesty and humility before the Lord and each of us showed the beauty of family life in all its richness and diversity. I pray that our days of prayer and reflection on the importance of the family for a healthy society will inspire families to continue to strive for holiness and to see the Church as their constant companion, whatever the challenges they may face.

At the end of my visit, I would also like to thank all those who prepared for my stay in the Archdioceses of Washington and New York. It was particularly moving for me to canonize St. Junípero Serra, who reminds us all of our call to be missionary disciples, and I was also very moved to stand with my brothers and sisters of other religions at Ground Zero, that place which speaks so powerfully of the mystery of evil. Yet we know with certainty that evil never has the last word, and that, in God's merciful plan, love and peace triumph over all.

Mr. Vice President, I ask you to renew my gratitude to President Obama and to the members of Congress, together with the assurance of my prayers for the American people. This land has been blessed with tremendous gifts and opportunities. I pray that you may all be good and generous stewards of the human and material resources entrusted to you.

I thank the Lord that I was able to witness the faith of God's people in this country, as manifested in our moments of prayer together and evidenced in so many works of charity. Jesus says in the Scriptures: "Truly, I say to you, as you did it to one of the least of these my brethren, you did it to me." Your care for me and your generous welcome are a sign of your love for Jesus and your faithfulness to him. So too is your care for the poor, the sick, the homeless, and the immigrant, your defense of life at every stage, and your concern for family life. In all of this, you recognize that Jesus is in your midst and that your care for one another is care for Jesus himself.

As I leave, I ask all of you, especially the volunteers and benefactors who assisted with the World Meeting of Families: do not let your enthusiasm for Jesus, his Church, our families, and the broader family of society run dry. May our days together bear fruit that will last, generosity and care for others that will endure! Just as we have received so much from God — gifts freely given us, and not of our own making — so let us freely give to others in return.

Dear friends, I embrace all of you in the Lord, and I entrust you to the maternal care of Mary Immaculate, Patroness of the United States. I will pray for you and your families, and I ask you, please, to pray for me. May God bless you all. God bless America!

XXXI

In-Flight Press Conference

PAPAL FLIGHT OF POPE FRANCIS FROM THE
UNITED STATES OF AMERICA TO ROME
SUNDAY, SEPTEMBER 27, 2015

~

Father Federico Lombardi
Your Holiness, we welcome you here. Thank you for once again taking time now after such a demanding and tiring journey. So we will get right to our questions. The first person is this young lady here, who wrote a piece about you for *Time* magazine, so she is well-informed about your visit to America. She will ask her question in English, and Matteo will translate it into Italian.

Pope Francis
Good evening, everyone, and thank you so much for your work, because you were all over the place! I was in the car, but you ... So thank you very much.

Elizabeth Dias
Thank you, Holy Father: I am Elizabeth Dias, correspondent for *Time* magazine. We are curious to know ... this was your first visit to the United States. What surprised you about the United States, and what differed from your expectations?

Pope Francis
Well, it was my first visit: I had never been here before. I was surprised by the warmth of the people, who were so kind: something beautiful but also different. In Washington, the welcome was warm but a little more formal; in New York, it was rather exuberant; in Philadelphia, it was very heartfelt. Three different expressions, but the same welcome! I was very struck by people's

kindness, by their welcome; and also in the religious ceremonies by their devotion, their sense of faith.... People could be seen praying, and this made a great impression on me. It's beautiful.

Dias
Was there any unexpected challenge from the United States? Any provocation?

Pope Francis
No, thank God, no, no.... Everything went well. No challenges. No provocations. Everyone was very polite. Nothing offensive, no negative things. But as for challenges, we keep working with these faithful people, as in the past, helping them to grow, being there for them in good times and in bad, amid hardships, when there is no work, amid sickness.... The challenge for the Church today is what it always has been: to be close to people, close to people in the United States, not to be a Church cut off from people ... but close. And this is a challenge which the Church in the United States recognizes and is working at.

Father Lombardi
The second question is from David O'Reilly of the *Philadelphia Inquirer*, one of the major papers in Philadelphia, where we have been these days.

David O'Reilly
Holy Father, Philadelphia, as you know, has passed through a painful period with sexual abuse; it's still an open wound in Philadelphia. I know that many people in Philadelphia were surprised that in your address to the bishops, in Washington, you offered them encouragement and support. I think that many people in Philadelphia would like to ask you: "Why did you feel the need to offer the bishops encouragement and support?"

Pope Francis
In Washington, I spoke to all the bishops of the United States; they were all there, from the whole country. I felt the need to express empathy, because something really terrible took place, and many of them suffered because they weren't aware of it, or when

it came out, they suffered, as men of the Church, men of prayer, true pastors.... And I said that I knew that they — I used a word from the Bible, from the Book of Revelation: "You are coming from the great tribulation." What happened was a great tribulation. But not only emotional suffering. This is what I said today to those who suffered abuse. It was ... I won't say *apostasy*, but almost a *sacrilege*. We know that abuse is everywhere: in families, in neighborhoods, in schools, in gyms, everywhere. But when a priest commits abuse, it is extremely grave, because the vocation of the priest is to help that boy or girl to aim high, to grow in the love of God, to grow to affective maturity and goodness. And instead of that, he crushed them, which is evil. That is why it is practically a sacrilege. He betrayed his vocation, the Lord's call. That is why the Church is now working hard on this. These things must not be covered up; and those who covered them up are also guilty, even some bishops who covered them up. It is a terrible thing. My words of support were not intended to say: "Don't worry about it; it's nothing!" They were more like: "This was so terrible that I imagine that you wept greatly over it." That was the sense of my words. And I had strong words today.

Father Lombardi

Thank you very much. Now I ask Maria Antonietta Collins and Andrés Beltramo Alvarez to approach for the next questions.

Maria Antonietta Collins

Holy Father, you have spoken a great deal about forgiveness, how God forgives us, and how we are the ones who often have to ask forgiveness. I would like to ask you, after having seen you today at the seminary: there are many priests who sexually abused minors and have not asked forgiveness from their victims. Do you forgive them? And do you understand, on the other hand, the victims and their relatives who cannot, or do not want, to forgive?

Pope Francis

If a person has done wrong, and is conscious of what he has done, but does not beg forgiveness, I ask God to take this into account. I forgive him, but he does not accept forgiveness, he is closed to forgiveness. It is one thing to forgive – we are bound to forgive, because we have all been forgiven – but it is another thing to accept forgiveness. If that priest is closed to forgiveness, he will not receive it, because he has locked the door from the inside; all that remains is to pray that the Lord will open that door. We must be ready to forgive, but not all can receive it or are able or willing to receive it. What I'm saying is harsh. But this explains why some people finish their lives badly, without receiving God's tender mercy. And your second question?

Collins

Whether you understand victims and relatives who find themselves unable to forgive, or who do not want to forgive?

Pope Francis

Yes, I understand them. I understand them, I pray for them, and I do not judge them. Once, in one of these meetings, I met several people, and one woman said to me: "When my mother found out that I had been abused, she blasphemed God; she lost her faith and died an atheist." I understand that woman. I understand her, and God, who is better than I am, understands her. I am certain that God has welcomed that woman, because what was touched, what was destroyed, was her own flesh, the flesh of her daughter. I understand that. I do not judge someone who cannot forgive. I pray and I ask God, because God is a master at finding a way to resolve things. I ask him to take care of it.

Father Lombardi

Andrés Beltramo, of *Notimex*, who will perhaps ask his question in Italian; that way it helps all of us.

Andrés Beltramo

Father, thank you, first of all, for this moment. We have all heard you speak so much about the peace process in Colombia, between FARC and the government. Now there is a historic agreement. Do you feel somehow a part of this agreement? You have also said that you were thinking of going to Colombia when this agreement would come about: there are many Colombians who now expect you.... One other little question: How do you feel after such an intense trip, once the airplane takes off? Thank you, Father.

Pope Francis
First, when I heard the news that the agreement would be signed in March, I said to the Lord: "Lord, help us reach March; help us get there with this beautiful wish, because some small things still have to be done, but the will is there. On both sides. It is there. Even on the part of the small group, all three are in agreement. We have to reach March for the definitive accord. That was the point of international justice, as you know. I was very pleased. And I feel like I was part of it in the sense that I have always desired this, and I spoke twice with President [Juan Manuel] Santos about the problem. And the Holy See ... not just myself, but the Holy See is very willing to help as much as possible.

The other thing. This is a bit personal, but I have to be honest. When the plane leaves after a visit, I think of the faces of all those people. I get the urge to pray for them and to say to the Lord: "I came here to do some good; perhaps I have done wrong, forgive me. But watch over all those people who saw me, who thought about the things I said, who heard me, even those who criticized me, all of them...." This is what I feel. I don't know. That's what I feel. But it's a bit — sorry — personal: you can't say this in the newspapers....

Father Lombardi
Thank you very much. Thomas Jansen of CIC, the German Catholic Agency.

Thomas Jansen
Holy Father, I wanted to ask about the immigrant crisis in Europe. Many countries are building new fences out of barbed wire. What do you think about this development?

Pope Francis

You used a word: "crisis." A state of crisis comes about as the result of a long process. This is a process which has been brewing for years, because the wars which those people are fleeing have been going on for years. Hunger. Hunger has been going on for years. When I think of Africa — this is a bit simplistic, but I give it as an example — I get to thinking: Africa, the exploited continent. They went after slaves there, and then so many resources. The exploited continent. And now, wars, tribal and not, have economic interests behind them. And I think that, rather than exploiting a continent or a nation or a land, invest there, so that those people can have work and the crisis can be avoided. It is true: this is a refugee crisis — as I said in the Congress — unprecedented since the aftermath of World War II, the largest of them. You ask me about fences, walls. You know what happens to walls, all of them. Walls all fall down — today, tomorrow or in a hundred years — but they will fall. Building walls is not a solution; a wall is not a solution. Europe is presently in difficulty, this is true. We have to think; we have to understand why this great wave of migration is taking place, and it is not easy to come up with solutions. But dialogue among countries, that is how solutions can be found. Walls are never solutions, but bridges always are. I don't know. What do I think about walls and the barriers … whether they last for a short or a long time … they are not a solution. The problem remains, and hatred grows. That's what I think.

Father Lombardi

Jean-Marie Guénois of *Figaro*, from the French group.

Jean-Marie Guénois

Holy Father, obviously you cannot anticipate the debates of the synod fathers; we realize that, but we want to know before the synod if in your heart as a pastor, you really want a solution for the divorced and remarried. We also want to know if your *motu proprio* on the easing of the annulment process has, to your mind, closed this debate. Finally, how do you respond to those who fear that this reform has de facto created "Catholic divorce"? Thank you.

Pope Francis

I'll start with the last question. In the reform of the procedures and means, I closed the door to the administrative process, which was the way that divorce could have crept in. You could say that those who are thinking of "Catholic divorce" are mistaken because this latest document closed the door to divorce. It would have been easier with the administrative process. There will always be the judicial process. Then, to continue with your third question: the document ... I don't remember if it was the third but you can correct me ...

Guénois

The question was on the idea of "Catholic divorce," whether the *motu proprio* has closed debate on the matter in the synod?

Pope Francis

This was something called for by the majority of the fathers in the synod last year: a streamlining of the process since some cases could last ten or fifteen years. There is one sentence, then another, there is one appeal, followed by another. It never ends. The double sentence, in cases where the first sentence was valid and not appealed, was introduced by Pope Benedict XIV, because in central Europe (I won't say which country), there were abuses, and to stop this he had introduced this, but it is not essential to the process. Procedures change, jurisprudence changes, it constantly improves. At the time there was a need to do this. Later, Pius X wanted to streamline (the process); he started, but he didn't have the time or opportunity to continue. The synod fathers asked that the procedures of marriage nullity be streamlined. I will leave it at that. The *motu proprio* speeds up the procedures, but it is not divorce, because a sacramental marriage is indissoluble. This is not something the Church can change. It is doctrine; as a sacrament, marriage is indissoluble.

The legal process for establishing that what seemed to be a sacrament was not, because of lack of freedom, for example, or lack of maturity, or mental illness.... There are any number of reasons that, after careful investigation, lead to the conclusion that there was no sacrament in a given case. For example, because the person was not free. Another example: now it's less common, but in some sectors of society it was common, at least in Buenos Aires, that when the fiancée got pregnant, they were told they had to get married. In Buenos Aires, I strongly urged, I practically forbade, my priests to celebrate such "shotgun" marriages. They take place to keep up appearances. Then the babies are born and some marriages work out, but there's no freedom. And then things go wrong, they separate: "I was forced to get married because I had to cover up the situation." This is a cause for nullity. There are many others; you can find (a list of) them on the Internet; they are all there.

Then there is the issue of second marriages, the divorced who enter a new union. Read what is in the *instrumentum laboris,* what is up for discussion. It seems to me somewhat simplistic to state that the synod ... that the solution for these people is for them to receive communion. That is not the only solution ... no. What the *instrumentum laboris* proposes is much more. The problem of new unions on the part of the divorced is not the only problem. The *instrumentum laboris* mentions many others. For example, young people are not getting married. They don't want to get married. This is a pastoral problem for the Church. Another problem: the affective maturity needed for marriage. Still another problem is faith: "Do I really believe that this is forever?" "Yes, yes, I believe ... " but do you really believe it? The preparation for a wedding ... I often think that the preparation for becoming a priest takes eight years, and then, it is not definitive; the Church can remove the clerical state. But for marriage, which is for life, we offer four courses, four meetings.... Something is not right. The synod will have to consider carefully how to prepare couples for marriage. This is one of the hardest things. There are many problems; these are all listed in the *instrumentum laboris.* I am glad you asked about "Catholic divorce." No, it doesn't exist. Either there was no marriage — and this is nullity, that it did not exist — or, if there was a marriage, it is indissoluble. This is clear. Thank you.

Father Lombardi
Thank you, Holy Father. Now it is the turn of Terry Moran of ABC News, one of the great American networks.

Terry Moran
Holy Father, thank you very much, and thanks to the Vatican staff as well. Holy Father, you visited the Little Sisters of the Poor, and we were told that you wanted to show your support for the Sisters, also in their court case. Holy Father, do you also support those individuals, including government officials, who say they cannot in good conscience, their personal conscience, comply with certain laws or carry out their duties as government officials, for example in issuing marriage licenses to same-sex couples? Would you support those claims of religious freedom?

Pope Francis
I can't foresee every possible case of conscientious objection. But yes, I can say conscientious objection is a right, and enters into every human right. It is a right, and if a person does not allow for conscientious objection, he or she is denying a right. Every legal system should provide for conscientious objection because it is a right, a human right. Otherwise, we would end up selecting between rights: "This right is good, this one less so." It is a human right. I am always moved when I read, and I have read it many times, when I read the *Chanson de Roland*, when there were all these Moors lined up before the baptismal font, and they had to choose between baptism and the sword. They had to choose. They weren't permitted conscientious objection. It's a right and if we want to have peace, we have to respect all rights.

Moran
Would that include government officials as well?

Pope Francis
It is a human right. And if a government official is a human person, he enjoys that right. It is a human right.

Father Lombardi
Thank you. Now it is the turn of Stefano Maria Paci, of the Italian group Sky News.

Stefano Maria Paci
Your Holiness, at the [United Nations] you used very strong words to denounce the world's silence before the persecution of Christians who are deprived of their homes and goods, driven out, enslaved, and brutally murdered. Yesterday, President [François] Hollande announced that France has started bombing ISIS bases in Syria. What do you think of this military action? Also, out of curiosity: Mayor [Ignazio] Marino, the mayor of Rome, the city of the Jubilee, stated that he came to the World Meeting of Families because you invited him. Can you tell us how it went? [Note: Roman authorities have clarified that Mayor Marino never claimed to have been invited by the Holy Father.]

Pope Francis
I will start with your second question. I did not invite Mayor Marino. Is that clear? I did not invite him, and I asked the organizers, and they didn't invite him either. He came. He says he is a Catholic, and he came of his own accord. That's what happened. The first thing.

The other question was about bombings. Actually, I heard the news the day before yesterday, and I haven't read anything about it. I don't know much about the situation. I heard that Russia has taken one position, and that of the United States was not yet clear. I don't know what to say because I haven't fully understood the situation. But when I hear the word "bombing," death, bloodshed … I repeat what I said to Congress and at the UN: these things are to be avoided. But I don't know. I can't judge the political situation because I am not familiar with it. Thank you.

Father Lombardi
Thank you. Now Miriam Schmidt of Deutsche Presse-Agentur.

Miriam Schmidt

Holy Father, I wanted to ask a question about the relationship of the Holy See with China and the situation in that country, which is quite difficult also for the Catholic Church. What are your thoughts?

Pope Francis

China is a great nation which offers the world a great culture and so many good things. I once said as we were flying over China, returning from Korea, that I would very much like to go to China. I love the Chinese people, I wish them well, and I hope for a possibility of good relations. We do have contacts, we talk, we are moving forward, but for me, having as a friend a country like China, which has a great culture and such opportunity to do good, would be a joy.

Father Lombardi

Thank you. And now we have Sagrario Ruiz de Apodaca.

Sagrario Ruiz de Apodaca

Thank you. Good evening, Holy Father. You visited the United States for the first time, never having been there before, you spoke to Congress and the United Nations, and you drew great crowds. Do you feel more powerful? I would also like to ask you, because we heard you speak about the role of religious women and women in the Church in the United States: Will we ever see women priests in the Catholic Church, as some groups in the United States are demanding and as is the case in some other Christian churches?

Pope Francis

The Sisters in the United States have done wonders in the areas of education and health care. People in the United States love the Sisters. I don't know how much they may love the priests, but they do love the sisters. They are good women, very good women. Each follows her own congregation and its rules; there are differences, but they are good. and for this reason I felt bound to thank them for what they have done. An important person in the

United States government told me in these days: "Whatever education I received, I owe above all to the sisters." The sisters have schools in all neighborhoods, rich and poor. They work with the poor in hospitals.... This was the first question. I remember the third one, but the second?

Ruiz de Apodaca
Whether you feel powerful after being in the United States, with this agenda and being so successful ...

Pope Francis
I don't know if I was successful or not. But I'm afraid of myself. Because if I am afraid of myself, I always feel, I don't know, weak in the sense of powerless. Power is also fleeting, here today, gone tomorrow.... It's important if you can do good with power. Jesus defined power: true power is service, serving others, serving the poor. And I still have to advance on this path of service, because I feel that I don't do everything I must do. That is how I feel about power.

Third, on women priests, this cannot be done. Pope St. John Paul II, when the question was being raised, after very lengthy reflection, stated this clearly. Not because women aren't capable, but ... look, in the Church, women are more important than men, because the Church is a woman. We speak of the Church as "she"; she is the Bride of Christ. And Our Lady is more important than popes, bishops, and priests. I must acknowledge that we are somewhat behind in the developing of theology of women. We have to progress in that area. That is certainly true. Thank you.

Father Lombardi
Now the last question is from Matilde Imbertì, of Radio France, and then we finish.

Matilde Imbertì
Holy Father, in the United States you became a celebrity. Is that good for the Church, that the pope is a celebrity?

Pope Francis

Do you know what title the popes used to use, and should still use? "Servant of the servants of God." That is a little different than being a celebrity, a "star." Stars are beautiful to gaze at. I like to gaze at them in the summer, when the sky is clear. But the pope must be, has to be, the servant of the servants of God. In the media this sort of thing happens. But there is another side to the story. How many stars have we seen shine, then go out and fall. It is something fleeting. Whereas being the servant of servants of God, that is something beautiful. It doesn't pass away. That is what I think.

Father Lombardi

Good. We have come to the end of the list ... many thanks for your availability. We have had about fifty minutes of conversation, which has been a fair amount of time. Congratulations on the endurance you have shown throughout this journey and in this conversation with us. We will continue to follow you. It doesn't end with this journey. This visit has concluded, but we have the synod and so many other things.... And we want to keep following you with great affection, esteem, and appreciation, in the hope of assisting you in your service of the servants of God.

Pope Francis

Thank you for your work, for your patience, your kindness. Thank you. I am at your service. I pray for you, I do. Thanks for your help. Have a good flight!